Principles and Standards for School Mathematics Navigations Series

NAVIGATING
through NUMBER
and
OPERATIONS
in
PREKINDERGARTEN–
GRADE 2

Mary Cavanagh
Linda Dacey
Carol R. Findell
Carole E. Greenes
Linda Jensen Sheffield
Marian Small

Carole E. Greenes
Prekindergarten–Grade 2 Editor
Peggy A. House
Navigations Series Editor

NATIONAL COUNCIL OF
TEACHERS OF MATHEMATICS

The National Council of Teachers of Mathematics is a public voice of mathematics education, providing vision, leadership, and professional development to support teachers in ensuring mathematics learning of the highest quality for all students.

Printed in the United States of America

TABLE OF CONTENTS

Contents of the CD-ROM

Applets

Concentration
Frames

Blackline Masters

Templates for Pattern Blocks

Readings from Publications of the National Council of Teachers of Mathematics

About This Book

Navigating through Number and Operations in Prekindergarten–Grade 2 is the first of four grade-band books that demonstrate how teachers can introduce, develop, and extend some important ideas of number and operations. The introduction to this book gives an overview of the development of number and operations concepts from prekindergarten through grade 12. The three chapters that follow the introduction focus on some basic ideas of number or operations. Chapter 1 deals with counting, ordering, and representing numbers; chapter 2 introduces simple meanings of addition, subtraction, multiplication, and division; and chapter 3 introduces basic fact strategies and develops ideas about estimation, and computation related to addition and subtraction.

Each chapter begins with a discussion of the foundational ideas and the expectations for students' accomplishments by the end of grade 2. This discussion sets the stage for student activities that introduce and promote familiarity with the basic ideas. Each activity begins by identifying the recommended grade levels and presenting a summary of the activity. The goals that students are to achieve, the prerequisite knowledge and skills, and the necessary materials follow. Blackline masters, signaled in the text by an icon and identified in the materials lists, appear in the appendix. They are also available on the CD-ROM that accompanies the book. The CD, also signaled by an icon, contains two applets for students to manipulate and resources for teachers' professional development.

All activities follow the same format. Each consists of three sections: "Engage," "Explore," and "Extend." The "Engage" section presents tasks to capture students' interests. "Explore" presents the core investigation that all students should be able to do. "Extend" offers additional activities for students who demonstrate continued interest and want to do some challenging mathematics. Throughout, the activities present questions that teachers can pose to stimulate students to think more deeply about the mathematical ideas. Possible responses appear in parentheses after some questions. Margin notes include teaching tips and resources, students' work, and quotations from *Principles and Standards for School Mathematics* (National Council of Teachers of Mathematics 2000). The discussion for each activity identifies connections with other content strands in the curriculum and with process strands, offers insights about students' performance, and suggests ways to modify the activities for students who are experiencing difficulty or who need greater challenge. Teachers can modify most of the activities for use by students at any grade level in the pre-K–2 grade band. To make adjustments that will most enhance students' learning, teachers should observe students' performance, taking note of the appropriateness of their mathematical vocabulary, the clarity of their explanations, the robustness of their rationales for their solutions, and the complexity of their creations.

A cautionary note: This book does not offer a complete curriculum for number and operations in this grade band. Rather, teachers should use it in conjunction with other instructional materials.

Key to Icons

Principles and Standards

Blackline Master

CD-ROM

Three different icons appear in the book, as shown in the key. One alerts readers to material quoted from *Principles and Standards for School Mathematics,* another points them to supplementary materials on the CD-ROM that accompanies the book, and a third signals the blackline masters and indicates their locations in the appendix.

Pre-K–Grade 2

Navigating through Number and Operations

Introduction

What could be more fundamental in mathematics than numbers and the operations that we perform with them? Thus, it is no surprise that Number and Operations heads the list of the five Content Standards in *Principles and Standards for School Mathematics* (NCTM 2000). Yet, numbers and arithmetic are so familiar to most of us that we run the risk of underestimating the deep, rich knowledge and proficiency that this Standard encompasses.

Fundamentals of an Understanding of Number and Operations

In elaborating the Number and Operations Standard, *Principles and Standards* recommends that instructional programs from prekindergarten through grade 12 enable all students to—

- understand numbers, ways of representing numbers, relationships among numbers, and number systems;
- understand meanings of operations and how they relate to one another;
- compute fluently and make reasonable estimates.

The vision that *Principles and Standards* outlines in the description of this Standard gives Number and Operations centrality across the entire mathematics curriculum. The *Navigating through Number and Operations* volumes flesh out that vision and make it concrete in activities for students in four grade bands: prekindergarten through grade 2, grades 3–5, grades 6–8, and grades 9–12.

Understanding numbers, ways of representing numbers, relationships among numbers, and number systems

Young children begin to develop primitive ideas of number even before they enter school, and they arrive in the classroom with a range of informal understanding. They have probably learned to extend the appropriate number of fingers when someone asks, "How old are you?" and their vocabulary almost certainly includes some number words. They are likely to be able to associate these words correctly with small collections of objects, and they probably have been encouraged to count things, although they may not yet have mastered the essential one-to-one matching of objects to number names. During the years from prekindergarten through grade 2, their concepts and skills related to numbers and numeration, counting, representing and comparing quantities, and the operations of adding and subtracting will grow enormously as these ideas become the focus of the mathematics curriculum.

The most important accomplishments of the primary years include the refinement of children's understanding of counting and their initial development of number sense. Multiple classroom contexts offer numerous opportunities for students to count a myriad of things, from how many children are in their reading group, to how many cartons of milk their class needs for lunch, to how many steps they must take from the chalkboard to the classroom door. With experience, they learn to establish a one-to-one matching of objects counted with number words or numerals, and in time they recognize that the last number named is also the total number of objects in the collection. They also discover that the result of the counting process is not affected by the order in which they enumerate the objects. Eventually, they learn to count by twos or fives or tens or other forms of "skip counting," which requires that quantities be grouped in certain ways.

Though children initially encounter numbers by counting collections of physical objects, they go on to develop number concepts and the ability to think about numbers without needing the actual objects before them. They realize, for example, that five is one more than four and six is one more than five, and that, in general, the next counting number is one more than the number just named, whether or not actual objects are present for them to count. Through repeated experience, they also discover some important relationships, such as the connection between a number and its double, and they explore multiple ways of representing numbers, such as modeling six as six ones, or two threes, or three twos, or one more than five, or two plus four.

Young children are capable of developing number concepts that are more sophisticated than adults sometimes expect. Consider the prekindergarten child who explained her discovery that some numbers, like 2 and 4 and 6, are "fair numbers," or "sharing numbers," because she could divide these numbers of cookies equally with a friend, but numbers like 3 or 5 or 7 are not "fair numbers," because they do not have this property.

As children work with numbers, they discover ways of thinking about the relationships among them. They learn to compare two numbers to determine which is greater. If they are comparing 17 and 20, for example, they might match objects in two collections to see that 3 objects are "left over" in the set of 20 after they have "used up" the set of 17, or they might count on from 17 and find that they have to count three more numbers to get to 20. By exploring "How many more?" and "How many less?" young children lay the foundations for addition and subtraction.

Continual work with numbers in the primary grades contributes to students' development of an essential, firm understanding of place-value concepts and the base-ten numeration system. This understanding often emerges from work with concrete models, such as base-ten blocks or linking cubes, which engage students in the process of grouping and ungrouping units and tens. They must also learn to interpret, explain, and model the meaning of two- and three-digit numbers written symbolically. By the end of second grade, *Principles and Standards* expects students to be able to count into the hundreds, discover patterns in the numeration system related to place value, and compose (create through different combinations) and decompose (break apart in different ways) two- and three-digit numbers.

In addition, students in grade 2 should begin to extend their understanding of whole numbers to include early ideas about fractions. Initial experiences with fractions should introduce simple concepts, such as the idea that halves or fourths signify divisions of things into two or four equal parts, respectively.

As students move into grades 3–5, their study of numbers expands to include larger whole numbers as well as fractions, decimals, and negative numbers. Now the emphasis shifts from addition and subtraction to multiplication and division, and the study of numbers focuses more directly on the multiplicative structure of the base-ten numeration system. Students should understand a number like 435 as representing $(4 \times 100) + (3 \times 10) + (5 \times 1)$, and they should explore what happens to numbers when they multiply or divide them by powers of 10.

The number line now becomes an important model for representing the position of numbers in relation to benchmarks like 1/2, 1, 10, 100, 500, and so on. It also provides a useful tool at this stage for representing fractions, decimals, and negative integers as well as whole numbers.

Concepts of fractions that the curriculum treated informally in the primary grades gain new meaning in grades 3–5 as students learn to interpret fractions both as parts of a whole and as divisions of numbers. Various models contribute to students' developing understanding. For example, an area model in which a circle or a rectangle is divided into equal parts, some of which are shaded, helps students visualize fractions as parts of a unit whole or determine equivalent fractions.

Number-line models are again helpful, allowing students to compare fractions to useful benchmarks. For instance, they can decide that 3/5 is greater than 1/3 because 3/5 is more than 1/2 but 1/3 is less than 1/2, or they can recognize that 9/10 is greater than 7/8 because 9/10 is

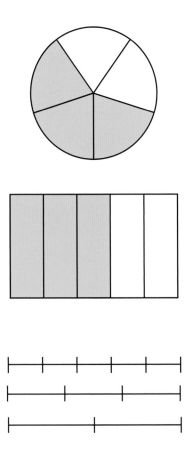

closer to 1 than 7/8 is. Parallel number lines, such as one marked in multiples of 1/3 and another in multiples of 1/6, can help students identify equivalences.

During these upper elementary years, students also encounter the concept of percent as another model for part of a whole. Their work should help them begin to develop benchmarks for common percentages, such as 25 percent, 33 1/3 percent, or 50 percent.

In grades 6–8, students expand their understanding of numbers to include the integers, and now they learn how to add, subtract, multiply, and divide with negative as well as positive numbers. Developing a deeper understanding of rational numbers is another very important goal for these students, who must increase their facility in working with rational numbers represented by fractions, decimals, and percents.

At this level, the curriculum places particular emphasis on developing proportional reasoning, which requires students to understand and use ratios, proportions, and rates to model and solve problems. Fraction strips, circles, number lines, area models, hundreds grids, and other physical models provide concrete representations from which students can draw conceptual meaning as they hone their understanding of rational numbers. Exposure to these models develops students' abilities to translate fluently from one representation to another, to compare and order rational numbers, and to attach meaning to rational numbers expressed in different but equivalent forms.

The concept of proportionality, which is a central component of the middle-school curriculum, serves to connect many aspects of mathematics, such as the slope of the linear function $y = mx$ in algebra, the scale factor in measurements on maps or scale drawings, the ratio of the circumference to the diameter of a circle (π) in geometry, or the relative frequency of a statistic in a set of data. Thus, students have numerous opportunities to develop and use number concepts in multiple contexts and applications. In some of those contexts, students encounter very large or very small numbers, which necessitate scientific notation and a sense of orders of magnitude of numbers.

Finally, students in grades 6–8 are able to focus more directly on properties of numbers than they were at earlier stages of development. They can investigate such key ideas as the notions of factor and multiple, prime and composite numbers, factor trees, divisibility tests, special sets (like the triangular and square numbers), and many interesting number patterns and relationships, including an introduction to some irrational numbers, such as $\sqrt{2}$.

When students move on to grades 9–12, their understanding of number should continue to grow and mature. In these grades, students customarily encounter many problems, both in mathematics and in related disciplines like science or economics, where very large and very small numbers are commonplace. In working such problems, students can use technology that displays large and small numbers in several ways, such as 1.219 E17 for 1.219 (10^{17}), and they need to become fluent in expressing and interpreting such quantities.

High school students also have many opportunities to work with irrational numbers, and these experiences should lead them to an understanding of the real number system—and, beyond that, to an understanding of number systems themselves. Moreover, students in grades 9–12 should develop an awareness of the relationship of those systems to various types of equations. For example, they should understand that the equation $A + 5 = 10$ has a whole-number solution, but the equation $A + 10 = 5$ does not, though it does have an integer solution. They should recognize that the equation $10 \cdot A = 5$ requires the rational numbers for its solution, and the equation $A^2 = 5$ has a real-number solution, but the equation $A^2 + 10 = 5$ is solved in the complex numbers.

Students should also understand the one-to-one correspondence between real numbers and points on the number line. They should recognize important properties of real numbers, such as that between any two real numbers there is always another real number, or that irrational numbers can be only approximated, but never represented exactly, by fractions or repeating decimals.

In grades 9–12, students also encounter new systems, such as vectors and matrices, which they should explore and compare to the more familiar number systems. Such study will involve them in explicit examination of the associative, commutative, and distributive properties and will expand their horizons to include a system (matrices) in which multiplication is not commutative. Using matrices, students can represent and solve a variety of problems in other areas of mathematics. They can find solutions to systems of linear equations, for instance, or describe a transformation of a geometric figure in the plane. Using algebraic symbols and reasoning, students also can explore interesting number properties and relationships, determining, for example, that the sum of two consecutive triangular numbers is always a square number and that the sum of the first N consecutive odd integers is equal to N^2.

Understanding meanings of operations and how operations relate to one another

As young children in prekindergarten through grade 2 learn to count and develop number sense, they simultaneously build their understanding of addition and subtraction. This occurs naturally as children compare numbers to see who collected more stickers or as they solve problems like the following: "When Tim and his dad went fishing, they caught seven fish. Tim caught four of the fish. How many did his dad catch?" Often, children use concrete materials, such as cubes or chips, to model "joining" or "take-away" problems, and they develop "counting on" or "counting back" strategies to solve problems about "how many altogether?" and "how many more?" and similar relationships.

Even at this early stage, teachers who present problems in everyday contexts can represent the problem symbolically. For example, teachers can represent the problem "How many more books does Emily need to read if she has already read 13 books and wants to read 20 books before the end of the school year?" as $13 + \square = 20$ or as $20 - \square = 13$. Such expressions help students to see the relationship between addition and subtraction.

Young children also build an understanding of the operations when they explain the thinking behind their solutions. For example, a child who had just celebrated his sixth birthday wondered, "How much is 6 and 7?" After thinking about the problem for a moment, he decided that $6 + 7 = 13$, and then he explained how he knew: "Well, I just had a birthday, and for my birthday I got two 'five dollars,' and my $5 and $5 are $10, so 6 and 6 should be 12, and then 6 and 7 must be 13."

As young students work with addition and subtraction, they should also be introduced to the associative and commutative properties of the operations. They should learn that when they are doing addition, they can use the numbers in any order, but they should discover that this fact is not true for subtraction. Further, they should use the commutative property to develop effective strategies for computation. For example, they might rearrange the problem $3 + 5 + 7$ to $3 + 7 + 5 = (3 + 7) + 5 = 10 + 5 = 15$.

Early work with addition and subtraction also lays the conceptual groundwork for later study of operations. Multiplication and division are all but evident when students repeatedly add the same number—for example, in skip-counting by twos or fives—or when they solve problems requiring that a collection of objects be shared equally among several friends. The strategies that young children use to solve such problems, either repeatedly adding the same number or partitioning a set into equal-sized subsets, later mature into computational strategies for multiplication and division.

The operations of multiplication and division, and the relationships between them, receive particular emphasis in grades 3–5. Diagrams, pictures, and concrete manipulatives play important roles as students deepen their understanding of these operations and develop their facility in performing them.

For example, if an area model calls for students to arrange 18 square tiles into as many different rectangles as they can, the students can relate the three possible solutions (1 by 18, 2 by 9, and 3 by 6) to the factors of 18. Similar problems will show that some numbers, like 36 or 64, have many possible rectangular arrangements and hence many factors, while other numbers, like 37 or 41, yield only one solution and thus have only two factors. By comparing pairs of rectangular arrangements, such as 3 by 6 and 6 by 3, students can explore the commutative property for multiplication. By decomposing an 18-by-6 area model, as illustrated in the three examples, students can develop an understanding of the distributive property.

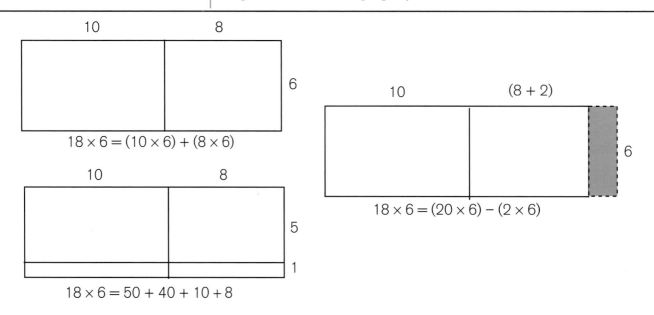

$$18 \times 6 = (10 \times 6) + (8 \times 6)$$

$$18 \times 6 = 50 + 40 + 10 + 8$$

$$18 \times 6 = (20 \times 6) - (2 \times 6)$$

Other models for multiplication might involve rates or combinations. In grades 3–5, a typical problem involving a rate might be "If 4 pencils cost 69¢, how much will a dozen pencils cost?" Problems involving combinations at this level are often similar to the following: "How many different kinds of meat-and-cheese sandwiches can we make if we have 2 kinds of bread (white and wheat), 4 kinds of meat (beef, ham, chicken, and turkey), and 3 kinds of cheese (Swiss, American, and provolone)?" (See the tree diagram below.)

To develop students' understanding of division, teachers should engage them in working with two different models—a partitioning model ("If you have 36 marbles and want to share them equally among 4 people, how many marbles should each person receive?") and a repeated-subtraction model ("If you have 36 marbles and need to place 4 marbles into each cup in a game, how many cups will you fill?"). Students should be able to represent both models with manipulatives and diagrams.

In exploring division, students in grades 3–5 will inevitably encounter situations that produce a remainder, and they should examine what the remainder means, how large it can be for a given divisor, and how to interpret it in different contexts. For example, arithmetically, 28 ÷ 5 = 5 3/5, but consider the solutions to each of the following problems:

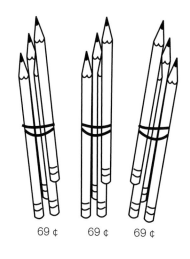

69 ¢   69 ¢   69 ¢

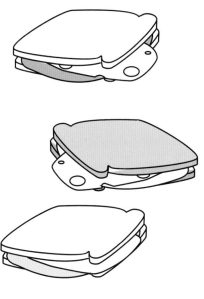

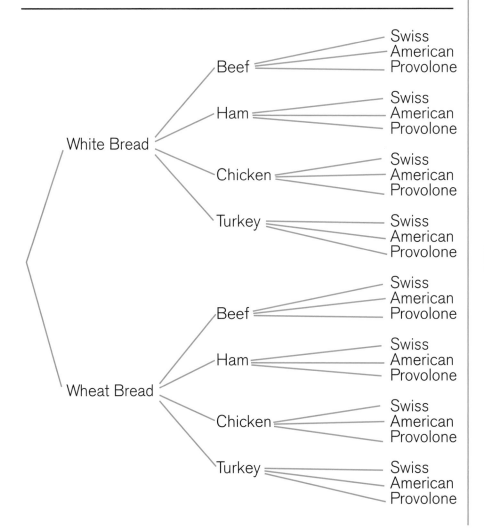

- "Compact disks are on sale for $28 for 5 disks. How much should one disk cost?" ($5.60)
- "Muffins are packaged 5 to a box for the bake sale. How many boxes can you make up if you bake 28 muffins?" (5).
- "Parents will be transporting children in minivans for the class field trip. Each van can take 5 children. The class has 28 children. How many vans will parents need to drive for the trip?" (6).

The understanding of all four operations that students build with whole numbers in the upper elementary grades broadens during grades 6–8, when they apply those operations to fractions, decimals, percents, and integers. Moreover, as students operate with rational numbers and integers, they encounter new contexts that may challenge their conceptual foundations. For example, when students are multiplying or dividing with fractions or decimals between 0 and 1, they see results that expose as misconceptions the commonly held beliefs that "multiplication makes larger" and "division makes smaller."

Other challenges that middle-grades students must confront include understanding when the result of a computation with integers is positive and when it is negative, knowing how to align decimals in computations with decimal fractions, and recognizing where in an answer to place a decimal point. Operating with fractions has proven difficult for many students. Lacking conceptual understanding, many have tried to get by with rote application of procedures that they don't understand. In the middle grades, therefore, it is important that students develop an understanding of the meaning of such concepts as numerator, denominator, and equivalent fractions and their roles in adding and subtracting fractions.

Middle school students need to model and compare expressions that are frequently subject to confusion, such as "divide by 2," "multiply by 1/2," and "divide by 1/2," and they must see that different models of division are sometimes required to give meaning to such ideas. For example, "divide by 2" can be modeled by a partitioning model ("separate the amount into two equal quantities"), but "divide by 1/2" is more appropriately represented by a repeated-subtraction model:

"You made $2\frac{3}{4}$ gallons of lemonade. How many $\frac{1}{2}$ -gallon bottles can you fill?"

$$\left(2\frac{3}{4} \div \frac{1}{2} = 5, \text{ with a remainder of } \frac{1}{4} \text{ gallon}\right)$$

Encouraging students to estimate and evaluate the reasonableness of the results of their computations is important in helping them expand their number sense.

As students' algebraic concepts grow during grades 6–8, they will also frequently face computations involving variables, and they will need to extend their understanding of the operations and their properties to encompass simplification of and operations with algebraic expressions. Understanding the inverse relationship between addition and subtraction, between multiplication and division, and between "square" and "square root" will be important in such tasks.

In grades 9–12, students should go beyond producing the results of specific computations to generalize about operations and their properties and to relate them to functions and their graphs. For example, they should describe and compare the behavior of functions such as $f(x) = 2x$, $g(x) = x + 2$, $h(x) = x^2$, or $j(x) = \sqrt{x}$. They should reason about number relations, describing, for instance, the value of $a \cdot b$ where a and b are positive numbers and $a + b = 50$. They should understand and correctly apply the results of operating with positive or negative numbers when they are working with both equations and inequalities.

In addition, high school students should learn to perform operations in other systems. They should find vector sums in the plane, add and multiply matrices, or use multiplicative reasoning to represent counting problems and combinatorics.

Computing fluently and making reasonable estimates

Although an understanding of numbers and the meanings of the various operations is essential, it is insufficient unless it is accompanied by the development of computational proficiency and a sense of the reasonableness of computational results. Computational skills emerge in the prekindergarten and early elementary years in conjunction with students' developing understanding of whole numbers and counting.

Young children's earliest computational strategies usually involve counting. As they think about number problems involving addition or subtraction, young students devise different solution schemes, and teachers should listen carefully to their students' explanations of these thinking strategies. Encouraging children to explain their methods and discussing different students' strategies with the class helps students deepen their understanding of numbers and operations and refine their computational abilities.

At first, young children rely heavily on physical objects to represent numerical situations and relationships, and they use such objects to model their addition and subtraction results. Over time, they learn to represent the same problems symbolically, and eventually they carry out the computations mentally or with paper and pencil, without needing the actual physical objects. Students should have enough experience and practice to master the basic one-digit addition and subtraction combinations, and they should combine that knowledge with their understanding of base-ten numeration so that, by the end of grade 2, they can add and subtract with two-digit numbers.

As students become more proficient with addition and subtraction, teachers can help them examine the efficiency and generalizability of their invented strategies and can lead them to an understanding of standard computational algorithms. When students understand the procedures that they are employing, they are able to carry them out with accuracy and efficiency.

In grades 3–5, students should extend their knowledge of basic number combinations to include single-digit multiplication and division facts, and by the end of the upper elementary years they should be able to compute fluently with whole numbers. As students develop their computational proficiency, teachers should guide them in examining and explaining their various approaches and in understanding algorithms for addition, subtraction, multiplication, and division and employing them effectively. In turn, teachers must understand that there is more than one algorithm for each of the operations, and they should recognize that the algorithms that are meaningful to students may not be the ones that have traditionally been taught or that some people have come to assume offer "the right way" to solve a problem.

In grades 3–5, students are beginning to work with larger numbers, and it is important for them to develop a strong sense of the reasonableness of a computational result and a facility in estimating results before computing. It will often be appropriate for students to use calculators when they are working with larger numbers. At other times, paper and pencil may be appropriate, or it may be reasonable for teachers to expect mental computation. Teachers and students should discuss various situations to assist students in developing good judgment about when to use mental arithmetic, paper and pencil, or technology for whole-number computation.

Other aspects of computational fluency in the 3–5 grade band involve understanding the associative, commutative, and distributive properties and seeing how those properties can be used to simplify a computation. Students at this level will also encounter problems that require the introduction of order-of-operations conventions.

While students in grades 3–5 are honing their skills with whole-number computation, they also will be spending a great deal of time developing an understanding of fractions and decimals. However, computing with rational numbers should not be the focus of their attention yet. Rather, students should apply their understanding of fractions and decimals and the properties of the operations to problems that include fractions or decimals. For example, "How many sheets of construction paper will Jackie need to make 16 Halloween decorations if each decoration uses 2 1/4 sheets of paper?" General procedures for calculating with rational numbers and integers will be the focus of instruction in the next grade band.

In grades 6–8, students learn methods for computing with fractions and decimals as extensions of their understanding of rational numbers and their facility in computing with whole numbers. As with whole-number computation, students develop an understanding of computing with fractions, decimals, and integers by considering problems in context, making estimates of reasonable expectations for the results, devising and explaining methods that make sense to them, and comparing their strategies with those of others as well as with standard algorithms. When calculating with fractions and decimals, students must learn to assess situations and decide whether an exact answer is required or whether an estimate is appropriate. They should also develop useful benchmarks to help them assess the reasonableness of results when they are calculating with rational numbers, integers, and percents. Computational fluency at the middle grades also includes a facility in reasoning about and solving problems involving proportions and rates.

In grades 9–12, students should extend their computational proficiency to real numbers and should confidently choose among mental mathematics, paper-and-pencil calculations, and computations with technology to obtain results that offer an appropriate degree of precision. They should perform complex calculations involving powers and roots, vectors, and matrices, as well as real numbers, and they should exhibit a well-developed number sense in judging the reasonableness of calculations, including calculations performed with the aid of technology.

Numbers and Operations in the Mathematics Curriculum

Without numbers and operations there would be no mathematics. Accordingly, the mathematics curriculum must foster the development of both number sense and computational fluency across the entire pre-K–12 continuum. The Number and Operations Standard describes the core of understanding and proficiency that students are expected to attain, and a curriculum that leads to the outcomes envisioned in this Standard must be coherent, developmental, focused, and well articulated across the grades. At all levels, students should develop a true understanding of numbers and operations that will undergird their development of computational facility.

The *Navigating through Number and Operations* books provide insight into the ways in which the fundamental ideas of number and operations can develop over the pre-K–12 years. These Navigations volumes, however, do not—and cannot—undertake to describe a complete curriculum for number and operations. The concepts described in the Number and Operations Standard regularly apply in other mathematical contexts related to the Algebra, Geometry, Measurement, and Data Analysis and Probability Standards. Activities such as those described in the four *Navigating through Number and Operations* books reinforce and enhance understanding of the other mathematics strands, just as those other strands lend context and meaning to number sense and computation.

The development of mathematical literacy relies on deep understanding of numbers and operations as set forth in the *Principles and Standards for School Mathematics*. These *Navigations* volumes are presented as a guide to help educators set a course for the successful implementation of this essential Standard.

NAVIGATING *through* NUMBER *and* OPERATIONS

Chapter 1
Counting, Ordering, and Representing Numbers

Young children's mathematical development begins long before they enter school. They construct an informal mathematical knowledge as they interact with others and with their environments. They count along with older siblings, parents, or other adults. They count small groups of objects and can often recognize the number of objects without counting. (This "seeing" of numbers is called *subitizing*.) They compare groups of objects and note which group has more.

Once they are in school, this informal knowledge expands and develops. Activities in this chapter build on this informal knowledge. They focus on counting in different ways, using concrete materials to explore place-value concepts, and representing whole numbers and fractions with a variety of models.

Counting and Ordering

Counting is a major component of the mathematics curriculum for young students. To be able to count successfully, students must know the word names for the numbers and be able to use them in the correct order. The repeating nature of the ones and tens digits in two-digit numbers facilitates counting to greater numbers. Initially, students count by ones. They then explore counting by other numbers, for example, by tens, fives, and twos. This "fancy" counting—usually called skip counting—serves as the basis for the introduction of multiplication.

Students learn to use counting to tell the number of objects in a set—that is, the *cardinality* of the set. To accomplish this type of counting, students must—

On the CD-ROM, see "Achievable Numerical Understandings for All Young Children" (Fuson, Grandau, and Sugiyama 2001) for specific mastery goals for numerical understanding for children aged three to seven.

- know that they can assign to each item in a set only one number from the number-word sequence;
- know that their count remains the same regardless of the size, shape, color, or function of objects, or the distance between any two objects;
- keep track of the items that they have counted;
- recognize that the last number word that they use in counting represents the total number of items in the set;
- understand that they can count objects in any order and the total remains the same.

Once they are able to count objects in a set, students compare sets to tell which has a larger (or smaller) number of objects and order the sets by numbers of objects.

In Choose a Number, students identify the number of objects in a group. They then explore how certain arrangements of objects can make counting easier to do.

In Counting in Different Ways, students review counting by ones. They learn to skip count by tens and by fives, and later by twos and by threes. They count by ones and clap or play a musical instrument on every number that is a multiple of 10. They follow the same procedure for multiples of 5 and then of 2 and 3. Finally they explore common multiples by, for example, clapping on multiples of 2 and tooting a recorder on multiples of 5. Both sounds occur simultaneously on 10, 20, 30, …, or the multiples of 10.

Students also count to identify the positions or locations of objects in a line or the events in a sequence. To identify position, students learn the ordinal numbers *first, second, third,* and so on. They can then tell that "Daniel is third in line" and that "Benita lives in the first house on the street."

Ducks in a Line introduces students to ordinal numbers. As they listen to the story *Make Way for Ducklings,* they represent the eight ducks in the story with objects and line them up. They then identify the position of each duck and the ducks who are *behind, in front of,* or *between* others.

Representations of Numbers and Place Value

Skill in counting and facility with counting numbers of objects in groups do not ensure that students understand the values of the digits in two- and three-digit numbers. That understanding develops as students engage in a variety of activities that involve regrouping place-value materials to go from ones to tens, tens to hundreds, and the reverse—tens to ones, and hundreds to tens. Through those actions, students learn that, for example, the 2 in 26 stands for 20, or two groups of ten. They come to realize that the order of the digits in a number is important. Although 26 and 62 contain the same digits, 62 is greater than 26 because it contains more tens. They also learn different ways to represent two-digit numbers.

In Trading Up or Down, students first explore the effect of adding 1 or 10 to two-digit numbers, then they identify the digit that will change, and ultimately they describe the nature of the change. For

See "The Influence of Language on Mathematical Representations" (Miura 2001) on the CD-ROM for more information on the effects of language on counting.

example, adding 10 to 47 will affect only the tens digit. Students then explore situations in which both digits change, as, for example, when they add 1 to 39.

In How Many Ways? students regroup place-value materials to explore different ways to represent two-digit and, later, three-digit numbers. They discover that, for instance, 34 can be represented as 3 tens and 4 ones, 2 tens and 14 ones, 1 ten and 24 ones, or 34 ones.

In All in Order, students form two-digit numbers and arrange them in order from least to greatest.

In Fraction Concentration, students are introduced to different ways to represent fractions. They play a game like Concentration, in which they have to match diagrams, word names, and symbols that all show halves, thirds, or fourths.

Expectations for Students' Accomplishments

By the end of grade 2, students should be able to count in a variety of ways. They should use counting to tell how many objects are in a group, and they should be able to compare groups to tell which has the greater or smaller number of members. They should use ordinal numbers to identify positions of objects in a line. When encountering two- or three-digit numbers, students should be able to apply place-value concepts and identify values of the digits, represent the numbers in different ways, and compare and order the numbers. Students should also be able to identify halves, thirds, and fourths of a whole and match word names and symbols to pictures showing parts of wholes.

See "Too Easy for Kindergarten and Just Right for First Grade" (Richardson 1997) on the CD-ROM for suggested quantities for students to estimate and count in kindergarten through grade 2.

Choose a Number

Kindergarten–Grade 1

Summary

Students explore a variety of representations for numbers.

Goals

- Recognize a variety of arrangements for a given quantity
- Use a variety of representations to model a number
- Represent numbers as sums and differences (optional)

Prior Knowledge

- Counting to 30 by ones

Materials

- Six round chips for each student
- Six square tiles for each student (optional)
- Drawing supplies (paper, pencils, crayons)
- Overhead projector (optional)

Activity

Engage

Give each student or pair of students six chips. On an overhead transparency or chalkboard, draw an arrangement of six large dots, two rows with three dots in each row. With the students' help, verify that the drawing represents the number 6. Have the students duplicate your arrangement with their chips. Make sure that students copy the arrangement correctly. Count the dots together from left to right. Then ask the students to find a different way to arrange the six counters, drawing a picture to show how they arranged them. Display the drawings around the room.

Have students identify the arrangement or arrangements that make it easy to see that the number of counters is six. Talk about why the others make it more difficult to see the number. For example, it is easy to tell that the arrangement of dots on the left side in figure 1.1 shows 6 (by skip counting the dots in rows by twos—2, 4, 6—or by skip counting the dots in columns by threes—3, 6). Take the opportunity to ensure

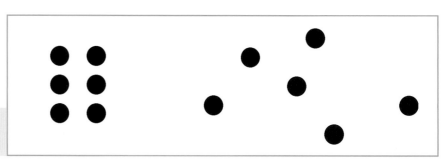

Fig. **1.1.**

Six dots

that the students also see the numeral (6) and the number word (*six*) for the number.

Explore

Display the drawings shown in figure 1.2. Tell the students that each one is another way to represent the same number. Ask them what number they think it is.

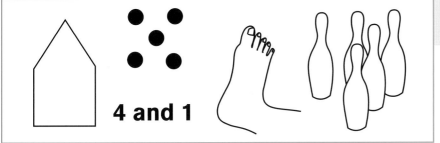

4 and 1

Fig. **1.2.**

Pictures for the number 5

Ask the students to think of other ways to represent the number 5, and then have them model, draw, or record their representations. Ensure that the students realize that representations such as 1 + 1 + 1 + 1 + 1, or 5 less than 10, or 2 and 2 and 1, or pictures that reflect the number 5 are all welcome. For more accomplished students, you may wish to require numerical representations involving addition or subtraction. Talk about the variety of representations that the students use. Challenge the students to generate as many ways to represent the number 5 as they can.

Have each student select a number from 10 to 30. Ask the students to find as many representations as possible for their number, drawing or writing several representations on one side of their paper and recording the numeral on the back side. Encourage them to include one incorrect representation for their classmates to discover.

Display the representations around the room, without showing the numerals written on the back. Name a number that one of the drawings represents and challenge the students to locate the drawing. Also have the students find the incorrect representation on that paper.

Extend

Each day, at the beginning of your mathematics session, you might begin by having the class or small groups find as many representations for a number as possible. To find a number to give to your students, you might use the date (for example, use 7 on October 7), the number of days that the students have been in school (use 28 on the twenty-eighth day of school), or a student's number choice.

Discussion

For a thorough understanding of number, students must recognize that different arrangements of the same quantity are equivalent and that any quantity can be described in a host of ways. The ability to understand and use some of the number principles, such as the commutative, distributive, and associative principles; facility with many of the strategies for mental computation; and—much later—the ability to solve algebraic equations are all dependent on an understanding of the equivalence of expressions. Any opportunity that you can give your students to develop numerical flexibility will benefit them in many mathematical situations.

Counting in Different Ways

Grades 1–2

Summary

First students begin with 1 and count by ones, and then they begin at some number other than 1 in the counting sequence and count on by ones. They do some "fancy" counting—that is, counting by twos, fives, tens, and threes. Using instruments to "sound" the multiples, they identify common multiples of pairs of numbers.

Goals

- Count by ones beginning with any number in the counting sequence
- Count by twos, fives, tens, and threes
- Identify common multiples

Prior Knowledge

- Counting by ones from 1 to 100
- Recognizing the numerals 1 through 30

Materials

- Number chart (1 to 100)
- Percussion instruments (tambourines, triangles, drums, or large plastic tubs) with drumsticks or thumping objects, recorders, or song flutes; three each of four different instruments
- Chalkboard or poster board

Activity

Conduct the activity with the entire class. Provide sufficient space for students to be seated or to stand in a circle.

Engage

Have your students stand in a circle and count by ones to 10 in unison. Call on students to do this in pairs and individually. Follow the same procedure for counting by ones from 1 to 20; then to 30, to 40, to 50, …, and to 100. Refer to a number chart as needed.

Give the students a starting number from 2 to 10, and have them count on by ones from that number. Repeat, using a starting number from 11 to 20. Always have students count in unison before they count in pairs or individually.

Explore

Seat your students in a circle. Demonstrate counting by tens to 100. Repeat, having the students say the numbers in unison with you. Repeat again, having the students clap their hands as they say each number.

Have the students count with you by ones from 1 to 100. On each number that is a multiple of 10, have the students clap their hands as they say the number.

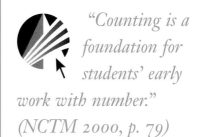

"Counting is a foundation for students' early work with number." (NCTM 2000, p. 79)

If students have difficulty counting on from a starting number other than 1, have them whisper the numbers from 1 to the starting number and then continue counting aloud after that.

Demonstrate counting by fives to 100. Have your students repeat the count with you, and then ask them to count again while clapping their hands as they say each number. Along with the students, count by ones to 100. On every number that is a multiple of 5, have students clap their hands. Follow the same procedure for counting by twos and by threes. Repeat these counting activities over a period of several weeks.

Extend

Have your students explore common multiples of 2 and 5 and of 2 and 3. To do this, give drums to three students and flutes or recorders to another three students. Tell the drummers that their job is to tap the drums every time the class says a number "that you'd say when you count by twos." Practice by having the class count from 1 to 30 with the drummers tapping their drums on 2, 4, 6, 8, …, 30.

Tell the students with flutes or recorders that their job is to blow one note (you can designate which hole on the flute or recorder to cover) every time the class says a number "that you'd say when you count by fives." Practice by having the class count from 1 to 30 with the flutes or recorders tooting on 5, 10, 15, …, 30.

Now have all the instrumentalists "play" together. As the class counts from 1 to 30, the drums will thump on multiples of 2 and the flutes or recorders will toot on multiples of 5. Do this twice. On the repeat, record the numbers on which *both* instruments simultaneously sound— that is, the numbers 10, 20, and 30. Draw the students' attention to the fact that these are the numbers that you say when you count by tens.

Follow the same procedure for the common multiples of 2 and 3. Count to 30. Use different instruments for the multiples of 2 and 3. Help your students discover that the common multiples of 2 and 3 are the numbers that they say when they count by sixes. You may also want to have students explore common multiples of 2 and 10, 3 and 10, or 5 and 10.

Discussion

Skip-counting activities like these are essential for preparing students for the study of multiplication. For example, students may use counting by twos to find the product of 4×2 by thinking, "I can count four twos—2, 4, 6, 8. So 4×2 is 8." They may find the product of 3×5 by thinking, "I can count three fives—5, 10, 15. So 3×5 is 15."

Finding numbers that are both "drummed" and "tooted" not only introduces students to common multiples but also sets the stage for later exploration of factors of numbers and the relationship between multiples and factors. For example, since 10 is a *multiple* of both 2 and 5, then 2 and 5 are both *factors* of 10.

There is a strong connection between the topic of patterns in the algebra strand and these activities that use counting patterns. To help students make the connection and see the patterns, you might want to have them color the multiples of 2, 3, 5, and 10 on a number chart, using a different color for each set of multiples. Common multiples would have two (or more) colors.

Some students may need a great deal of practice with counting. For these students, you may want to record the various counting sequences so that they can count along with an audiotape.

Ducks in a Line

Prekindergarten–Grade 1

Summary

The classic picture book *Make Way for Ducklings* (McCloskey 1941) sets the stage for an exploration of ordinal numbers. As students listen to the story, they repeat the order of the ducklings to identify the duckling that is *first* or *last*, or *between*, *before*, or *after* other ducklings.

Goals

- Identify position in a line by using the terms *first*, *second*, …, *eighth*, and *last*
- Identify people who are *between* others in a line
- Recognize that position is related to a point of view

Prior Knowledge

- Identifying people *in front of* and *behind* other people in a line

Materials

- *Make Way for Ducklings* (McCloskey 1941)
- Ducks cut from the blackline master "Eight Ducks"
- A copy of the blackline master "Eight Ducks" for each student

Activity

Engage

Arrange the students in a semicircle. Begin reading the story *Make Way for Ducklings* aloud. When you come to the part of the story where the ducklings hatch, pause after reading the following lines:

> One day the ducklings hatched out. First came Jack, then Kack, and then Lack, then Mack and Nack and Ouack and Pack and Quack.

Say, "Listen carefully to the names of the ducks as I read this part of the story again. Your job will be to tell me which duck hatched first, which hatched second, and so on." Reread the passage and ask, "Who hatched first?" (Jack) Read the passage again, and ask, "Who hatched second?" (Kack) Read the passage another time, and ask, "Who hatched last?" (Quack) Say, "I will read that part of the story again. This time count and tell me how many ducklings hatched." (8)

Explore

Place the eight ducks in the center of the reading circle. Call on students to read the names of the ducks with you. Help the students identify the initial

p. 88

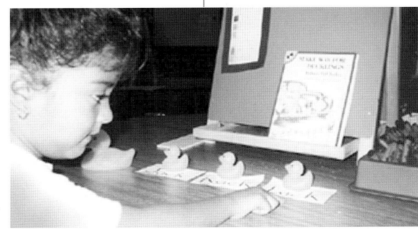

letter and name of each duck. Then say, "When the ducklings walked in a line, they walked in order. First came Jack, then Kack, then Lack, then Mack and Nack and Ouack and Pack and Quack." Help the students put the ducks in a line and in order. Ask questions about the relative positions of the ducks:

- "Who is first in line?" (Jack)
- "Who is third in line?" (Lack)
- "Who is last?" (Quack)
- "Who is between Kack and Mack?" (Lack)
- "Who is just behind Mack?" (Nack)
- "Who is fourth in line?" (Mack)
- "Who is in front of the line?" (Jack)

Place the eight ducks on the floor in front of the students. Call on students to name the ducks. Reread the story, allowing students to place the ducklings in order, forming a line. When you have finished the story, ask—

- "How many ducks are in front of Kack?" (One)
- "How many ducks are behind Quack?" (None)
- "How many ducks are in front of Nack?" (Four) "What are their names?" (Jack, Kack, Lack, and Mack)
- "How many ducks are behind Nack?" (Three) "What are their names?" (Ouack, Pack, and Quack)

Extend

Have students arrange the ducks in a different order and tell a new story that corresponds to the new order. Call on students to pose questions about which duck is first, second, last, after a particular duckling, before a particular duckling, or between two other ducklings.

You could also have your students construct a set of animals of their choice, place the animals in order, and pose questions about the order.

In each of the situations above, you could ask your students to reverse the line of animals so that the first becomes last and the last becomes first, and ask the same types of questions.

Alternatively, you could give your students a set of three to six animals, with clues about position, and have them place the animals in a line matching the clues.

Discussion

Make Way for Ducklings is an excellent book for prompting students to think about the relationships among elements in a sequence and how position designations (*first, second, last*) are related to a point of view. Having students line up for an activity or to leave the classroom and asking questions about who is first, second, or last will enhance their understanding of positional relationships.

Trading Up or Down

Grades 1–2

Summary

Students explore place value by examining how an increase or decrease of 1, 10, or 100 affects numerals for two-digit and three-digit numbers.

Goal

- Recognize how a number is affected by adding or subtracting 1, 10, or 100

Prior Knowledge

- Identifying the ones, tens, and hundreds digits of numbers
- Counting by tens
- Counting by hundreds
- Using base-ten blocks to represent two- and three-digit numbers

Materials

- Place-value materials such as base-ten blocks (10 ones-blocks, 10 tens-blocks, and 10 hundreds-blocks) for each pair of students
- A number cube numbered 1, 1, 1, 10, 10, 10 for each pair of students (for activity with two-digit numbers)
- A number cube numbered 1, 1, 10, 10, 100, 100 for each pair of students (for activity with two- and three-digit numbers)
- An operation cube (labeled +, +, +, –, –, –) for each pair of students
- Paper and pencils
- Calculators (optional)
- Overhead projector (optional)

Activity

Engage

Call on a student to name a two-digit number. Have all students model that number with their place-value materials (base-ten blocks, for example). Model the number on an overhead projector or the chalkboard after the students have completed their models. For example, if the number is 47, the base-ten block model would be as shown in figure 1.3.

Have each student add a ones-block to the arrangement and record the result. Ask questions about the changes to the number:

- "Which digit(s) changed?" "Why did it (they) change?" (added a ones-block)
- "Did any digit(s) not change?" "If so, why didn't it (they) change?" (added nothing)
- "How many ones-blocks would you have to add to make a tens digit change?" (depends on the ones digit)

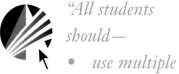

Base-Ten Blocks

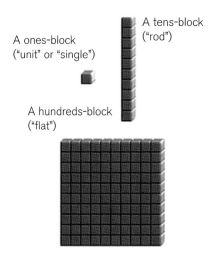

A ones-block ("unit" or "single")

A tens-block ("rod")

A hundreds-block ("flat")

Fig. **1.3.**

Base-ten model for 47

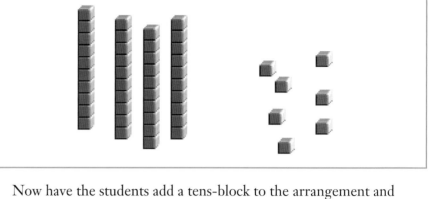

To create number and operation cubes, you can either use blank cubes and label the faces or cover the faces of dice with stickers that have been marked appropriately.

Now have the students add a tens-block to the arrangement and record the result. Ask questions about the changes to the number:

- "Which digit(s) changed?" "Why did it (they) change?" (added a tens-block)
- "Why didn't the ones digit change?" (The number of ones is the same as before.)

Have the students model the number 15 with one tens-block and five ones-blocks. Ask the students to add four ones-blocks to the collection representing 15, one at a time, recording as they count on from 15 to 19. Ask, "Which digit changed?" (ones digit) Now ask the students to add one more ones-block and make the necessary trade. Have the students talk about why both the tens digit and the ones digit changed when they added 1 to 19.

Begin again with, say, 55, represented by five tens-blocks and five ones-blocks. This time, count on by tens together as the students add four tens-blocks, one at a time, until they are modeling the number 95. Record the numbers that you say as you count the blocks. Guide the students to see that all the numerals have a 5 in the ones place and that only the tens digits are increasing. Depending on the experience of the students, you may wish to add an additional tens-block and make the necessary trade to a hundreds-block to show both the hundreds digit and the tens digit changing.

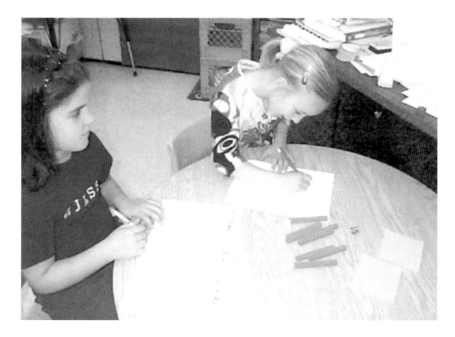

Repeat these activities to focus on subtraction, beginning with the number 55 and subtracting first ones-blocks and then tens-blocks, recording the resulting number each time.

Explore

Give each pair of students one operation cube and one of the number cubes. Reserve the cube marked with the numbers 1, 10, and 100 for students who are comfortable with three-digit numbers. Make sure that the students have paper and pencils for their work. Each student should choose a two-digit (or three-digit) number. The pairs of students then take turns rolling both the number cube and the operation cube and performing the required operation. For example, rolling a "+" and a 10 means that a student would add 10 to the starting number. Before giving the sum, the student must predict which digit(s) will change and what the new digit(s) will be. If the student is correct (as confirmed by a partner and verified with place-value models or a calculator), he or she uses the new value as a starting number for the next turn. If a student is not correct, his or her starting number does not change. The first student who arrives exactly at either 0 or 100 (with two-digit numbers) or 0 or 1000 (with three-digit numbers) wins the game.

Extend

A more challenging activity would require students to describe three different sets of rolls that would get them from one particular value to another. For example, to get from 304 to 400, they could roll one of the following:

Example 1: +100, −1, −1, −1, −1
Example 2: +10, +10, +10, +10, +10, +10, +10, +10, +10, +1, +1, +1, +1, +1, +1
Example 3: +100, +100, −10, −100, +10, +10, −1, −1, −1, −1, −10

Discussion

Although many students are adept at identifying digits in the ones, tens, and hundreds places of a number, this facility does not always translate into realizing how those digits change when a 1, 10, or 100 is added or subtracted. The activity Trading Up or Down helps students focus on these changes.

It is particularly at the transition points—from one ten to another, from one hundred to another, and from tens to hundreds (for example, from 94 to 104)—that students may struggle. It is important to watch students as they learn how to make the changes. Encourage students having difficulties to use base-ten blocks and do the required trading to visualize the transitions.

How Many Ways?

Grades 1–2

Summary

Using base-ten or Digi-Blocks, students model numbers between 10 and 100, identify ones and tens digits, and trade tens for ones to show different representations of the two-digit numbers. They record their findings and explore the number of different arrangements possible for a given number. They extend the explanation to three-digit numbers.

Goals

- Identify the values of the digits in two- and three-digit numbers
- Trade tens for ones and ones for tens
- Construct different representations of the same number

Prior Knowledge

- Counting to 100 by ones and by tens
- Recording numerals
- Modeling numbers with base-ten blocks

Materials

- Base-ten blocks or Digi-Blocks (at least 50 ones-blocks, 12 tens-blocks, and 2 hundreds-blocks for each student)
- Chart for recording possible groups of tens and ones

Activity

Engage

Give each student about forty ones-blocks. Record the numeral 32 on the chalkboard. Call on a student to name the number. Point to the 2. Have each student take that number of blocks to show them to you. Now point to the 3 in the numeral 32, and direct each student to take that many blocks. Note which students realize that they should take thirty blocks and which students take only three blocks. Choose a student who has chosen three blocks to explain that choice, and then choose a student who has chosen thirty blocks to explain that response.

Explore

Have each student count out 32 ones-blocks. (See fig. 1.4a.) Ask the students how they know they have exactly 32 blocks. (You will probably have to count them again to check.) Ask whether there is another way to show 32 with blocks. If students have experience working with the base-ten blocks, they may suggest that they could trade a group of 10 ones-blocks (or units) for 1 tens-block. If students do not suggest this on their own, you might demonstrate how easy it is to determine the number of blocks when they have been grouped as 3 tens-blocks and 2 ones-blocks. (See fig. 1.4b.)

"Using concrete materials can help students learn to group and ungroup by tens. For example, such materials can help students express '23' as 23 ones (units), 1 ten and 13 ones, or 2 tens and 3 ones."
(NCTM 2000, p. 81)

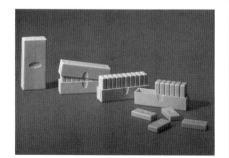

Digi-Blocks ™

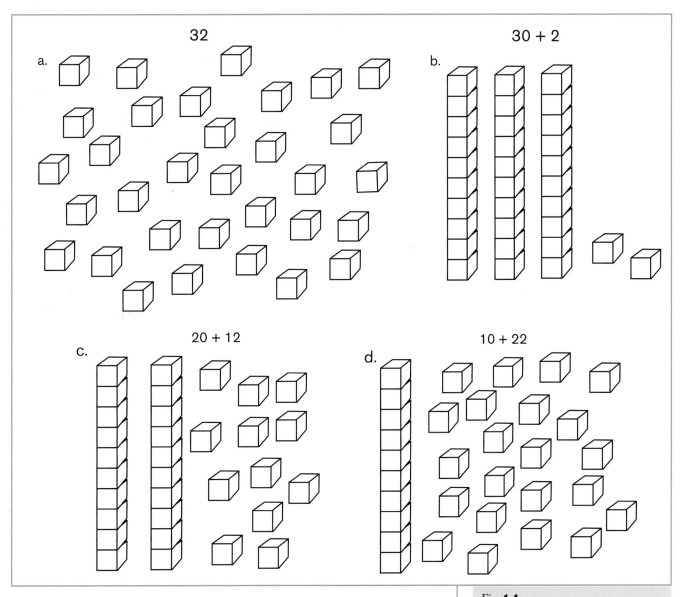

a. **32**

b. **30 + 2**

c. **20 + 12**

d. **10 + 22**

Fig. **1.4.**

Different representations of 32

Once the students have shown 32 as 32 ones-blocks and as 3 tens-blocks and 2 ones-blocks, ask, "Is there another way to show 32 with only tens-blocks and ones-blocks?" If students do not suggest both ways—2 tens-blocks and 12 ones-blocks or 1 tens-block and 22 ones-blocks—you might prompt them to look for additional ways. Have the students find all possible ways to show 32 with only tens-blocks and ones-blocks, and record their findings in a chart. Students should be able to find all the arrangements shown in figure 1.4.

Extend

Ask your students to predict the number of different ways of showing 43 with only tens-blocks and ones-blocks. After eliciting their predictions, give the students 43 ones-blocks and at least 10 tens-blocks. Also, give each student a chart such as the one that they used for their work with 32 for them to record their findings. Let the students record all the possibilities (4 tens-blocks, 3 ones-blocks; 3 tens-blocks, 13 ones-blocks; 2 tens-blocks, 23 ones-blocks; 1 ten-blocks, 33 ones-blocks; 43 ones-blocks). Ask if they have noted a pattern. (As the number of tens decreases, the number of ones increases by 10.) After working with several numbers in the same way, ask students to predict the number of different ways of showing numbers with tens-blocks and ones-blocks. (The number of arrangements will always be one more than the number of tens in the original number.)

If students are discovering all the different arrangements for numbers less than 100, you may want to challenge them to find different arrangements for numbers between 100 and 120. This will require careful organization and recording. Other questions to challenge students include the following:

- "Find a number that can be represented exactly seven ways using only tens-blocks and ones-blocks." (Any number in the 60s)
- "Show 45 with exactly eighteen blocks." (15 ones and 3 tens)
- "How many different numbers can you represent with exactly five blocks? List them." (50, 41, 32, 23, 14, 5)

Encourage your students to make up similar challenges for one another. You might want to write these on cards to leave in a learning center.

Discussion

When you ask your students to show you the number of blocks represented by the 3 in 32, do not be surprised if there are several students who choose only three ones-blocks. It is important to build a solid understanding of place value in the early grades, and students will need a variety of concrete tasks to do this. However, be aware that the use of physical models will not ensure that students understand the meaning of place value. Multiple tasks will make them reason about and discuss the meaning of the numbers.

These tasks are designed to help students build concepts about our base-ten numeration system by grouping and regrouping tens and ones. Not only are these concepts crucial to a solid understanding of the meaning of numbers and place value, but they also give a strong foundation for later work with addition and subtraction of two- and three-digit numbers.

"Using materials, especially in a rote manner, does not ensure understanding. Teachers should try to uncover students' thinking as they work with concrete materials by asking questions that elicit students' thinking and reasoning."
(NCTM 2000, p. 80)

All in Order

Grade 2

Summary

Students roll pairs of number cubes, use the numbers that are facing up to form two-digit numbers, and order the numbers from least to greatest.

Goal

- Compare and order two-digit numbers

Prior Knowledge

- Recognizing numerals up to 66

Materials

- A copy of the blackline master "'All in Order' Game Sheet" for each group of four students
- Number cubes numbered 1, 2, 3, 4, 5, 6; two for each group of students
- Base-ten blocks (optional)
- Index cards (at least four for each student)

Activity

Engage

Have your students sit in a circle. Show them the number cubes. Roll the cubes and point to the numerals showing on the tops. Tell the students that their job is to use these numerals to form a two-digit number. The numeral on one cube will be the tens digit, and the numeral on the other cube will be the ones digit. For example, if the two numerals are 2 and 5, the students can form two two-digit numbers—25 and 52. Roll the cubes and call on a student to name the numbers that he or she can form. Ask the students to compare the numbers and tell which is greater. Repeat this process several times. Ask the students if it is always possible to form two numbers. Guide them to realize that if the numerals on the two cubes are the same, they can form only one number (11, 22, …, 66).

Arrange the students in groups of three or four. Give each group a pair of number cubes. Have the students take turns rolling the cubes. You might consider asking them to write each number on an index card. The cards will make it easier and more enjoyable for the students to order the numbers later. After each roll, they should record all the two-digit numbers that they can form. Every student in a group should roll the cubes twice, and then the students should order their numbers from least to greatest.

When the students have completed this task, bring the class together and gather the cards or record all the numbers formed by the groups. Have the students order the numbers. Be sure that everyone understands

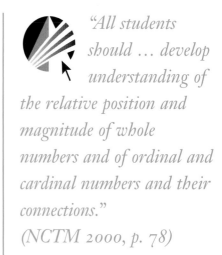

"All students should … develop understanding of the relative position and magnitude of whole numbers and of ordinal and cardinal numbers and their connections."
(NCTM 2000, p. 78)

p. 89

Have students model the numbers first with base-ten blocks. The block models will help them compare the numbers and order them from least to greatest and greatest to least.

how to compare numbers. Ask questions about possible numbers from rolling a pair of number cubes:

- "What is the smallest number that you could form?" (11) "How do you know?" (1 is the smallest number on each cube)
- "What is the greatest number that you could write?" (66) "How do you know?" (6 is the greatest numeral on each cube)
- "How many different numbers have 1 as the tens digit?" (Six) "How do you know?" (There are six numerals on each cube, so there are six possibilities: 11, 12, 13, 14, 15, 16)
- "How many different numbers have a tens digit of 6?" (Six) "How do you know?" (There are six numerals on each cube.)

Explore

Tell the students that they are going to play a little number game called "All in Order." Place the students in groups of four and give each group a pair of number cubes and a copy of the blackline master "'All in Order' Game Sheet." Let four students demonstrate the game before all the students play it on their own.

Have the first student roll the cubes, use the results as digits to form a two-digit number, and record that number in one of the four lines for round 1 on the game sheet. Explain how the student should decide which line to use:

- "If you think that your number is likely to be larger than the numbers that the three other students will form in their turns, you should write it on the fourth line."
- "If you think it is likely to be smaller than the numbers that the other students will form, you should write it on the top line."
- "If you think it is likely to be 'medium-sized' compared to the numbers that the other students will form, you should write it on one of the middle lines."

Have the second student roll the cubes, form a two-digit number, and record the number on one of the remaining three lines. In the same way, have the third and fourth students play.

Next, have the students record the four numbers in their correct order, from least to greatest, and compare the two lists of numbers to figure out their score. If they recorded all four numbers in the correct order, they get a group score of 4. If they placed only three of the numbers in the correct positions, their group score is 3, and so on. If they placed none of the numbers correctly, their group score is 0. A game consists of three rounds. The group's total score for a game is the sum of the scores for the three rounds.

Extend

You could extend this activity in two ways. First, the students could play the game with three number cubes, each numbered 1–6, and form and order three-digit numbers. Second, the students could investigate how many two- and three-digit numbers they could form with two and three number cubes, respectively. If your students work with two cubes, you should specify one cube to represent the tens digits and the other to represent the ones digits. Ask, "How many different numbers could we form?" (36) "How do you know?" Students can list and count the numbers, or they may reason as follows:

> "There are six different numbers that have a 1 in the tens place—11, 12, 13, 14, 15, 16. There are six different numbers that have a 2 in the tens place—21, 22, 23, 24, 25, 26. There are six different numbers that have a 6 in the tens place—61, 62, 63, 64, 65, 66."

The students could work with three number cubes in a similar manner.

Discussion

As students play the game "All in Order," they will become adept at comparing and ordering numbers. When your students bring their game sheets for you to check, be sure to identify students who are

If you want to specify one cube to represent the tens digit and one cube to represent the ones digit, you can use two cubes of different colors.

seldom able to order their list correctly. Play a one-on-one game with these students to help you discover where they need help.

This activity not only helps students learn to order two-digit numbers but also helps them think about the relative magnitudes of numbers to make the comparisons. As they play the game, students also develop strategies for placing the numbers on the lines that will give them the greatest chance for success. Encourage them to talk about their strategies.

Repeat this game throughout the year, varying it by changing the numerals on the number cubes or by increasing the number of cubes. You may want to introduce a zero on one cube and ask your students what numbers are possible when they roll a zero together with a nonzero number on the other cube—for example, 0 and 6. In this situation, they can form only one two-digit number (60). Explain to students that 06 is not a two-digit number. When zero is the only digit that precedes a nonzero number without a decimal point, we read the number as if the zero were not there. Thus, 06 is read as 6.

Fraction Concentration

Grades 1–2

Summary

Students play a game like Concentration, in which they match cards that show different representations of the same part of a whole.

Goals

- Identify halves, thirds, and fourths of a whole
- Identify models, symbols, and word names for 1/2, 1/3, and 1/4

Prior Knowledge

- Recognizing the difference between equal and unequal parts

Materials

- Copies of the blackline master "'Fraction Concentration' Cards" to make one set of cards for each pair of students
- Eight sheets of paper, with lines drawn to show equal or unequal regions, as in figure 1.5

The blackline master provides cards that you can cut out, paste on cardboard, and laminate.

p. 90

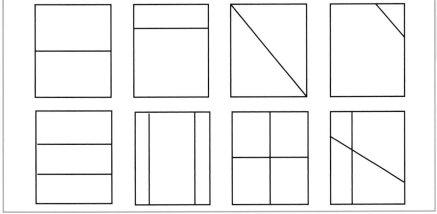

Fig. **1.5.**

Eight sheets of paper showing equal and unequal regions

Activity

Engage

Display one of the prepared sheets of paper. Ask the students to hold up their thumbs if the parts are equal. If the parts are not equal, they should hold their thumbs down. (See fig. 1.6.) Tape the papers with equal parts to the chalkboard.

"At this level, it is more important for students to recognize when things are divided into equal parts than to focus on fraction notation."
(NCTM 2000, p. 82)

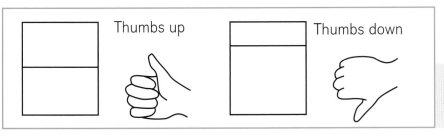

Thumbs up   Thumbs down

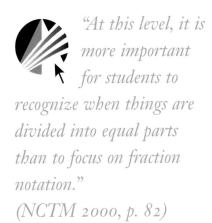

Fig. **1.6.**

Ask students to show with their thumbs whether the regions are equal or unequal

Explore

Distribute the "Fraction Concentration" cards to pairs of students. Have them sort the cards and describe the basis for their sorting. For instance, some may sort the cards into groups by name, picture, or number. Some students may even sort the cards by denominators: halves, thirds, fourths.

Tell the students that they are going to play a game called "Fraction Concentration." Explain how the game works:

- Players play in pairs.
- Players mix the cards and place them facedown in four rows with four cards in each row.
- Players take turns turning over two cards.
- If a player's cards match—that is, if they show the same fraction—the player keeps the cards and gets another turn. (See fig. 1.7.) If the cards don't match, the player replaces them facedown, and the other player takes a turn.
- When the players have taken all the cards, the game is over. The winner is the player with the greater number of cards.

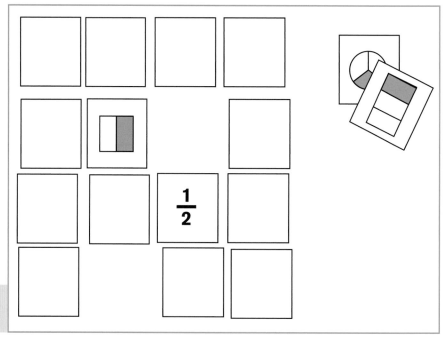

Fig. 1.7.

Playing "Fraction Concentration"

Extend

Display the three "Fraction Concentration" cards that show non-square rectangles with shaded parts. Have students look at the fractions and make *greater than* and *less than* comparisons. You may also want to display the "Fraction Concentration" circles, and ask your students to make the same types of comparisons.

Discussion

The first concept that children need to understand about fractional parts is that the parts must be equal in area. (Most models for young students, however, show parts that are congruent, equal in both size and shape.) An object divided into thirds has three equal parts. Point out

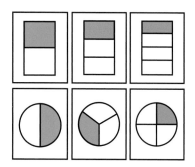

that fractions have "first names" and "last names." Have the students look again at the "Fraction Concentration" cards, and explain that the first name (numerator) of the fraction tells the number of parts that are shaded. The last name (denominator) tells the number of equal parts that the card shows. This first name–last name designation will help children later when they need to identify numerators and denominators to compare and compute with fractions.

For students who have difficulty identifying matching cards and dealing with the visual memory aspect of the game, play with the cards faceup. In that way, students can focus on the matching.

Conclusion

This chapter has introduced students to the concepts of counting, ordering, and representing numbers. Chapter 2 introduces students to the meanings of the four basic arithmetic operations—addition, subtraction, multiplication, and division.

"Ben's Understanding of One-Half" (Watanabe 1996; on the CD-ROM) reveals that a young child's understanding of one-half in one context is not necessarily related to his or her understanding of one-half in another context.

Students can reinforce their mathematical understandings and memory skills by working with the applet Concentration on the CD-ROM.

NAVIGATIONS
SERIES

PRE-K–GRADE 2

NAVIGATING *through* NUMBER *and* OPERATIONS

Chapter 2
Meanings of Operations

Young students are able to understand all four of the basic arithmetic operations if teachers introduce these operations in meaningful ways. In the early years, children can solve simple addition, subtraction, multiplication, and division problems if the contexts associated with the problems reflect real experiences and can be modeled with concrete materials.

Addition and Subtraction

The first operation that most students meet, and the easiest for most, is addition. The concept of joining and counting to find the total seems to be one with which children have some natural facility (Ginsburg, Klein, and Starkey 1998). Subtraction usually comes next, often very soon after addition. Although addition is always associated with some idea of combining, subtraction has a number of meanings that all seem different, at least on the surface. Often subtraction represents taking away (or separating), but just as often it is about comparing to determine how much more one quantity is than another. Subtraction often involves figuring how many are in one part if the other part and the total are known, or finding out how much more is needed to reach a specified total.

Researchers (e.g., Carpenter et al. 1999) often regard addition and subtraction situations as falling in different categories:

- "Join problems" (e.g., "Two people are in the room, and 2 more come in. How many are there altogether?")

- "Separate problems" (e.g., "Four people are in the room, and 2 leave. How many are still in the room?")
- "Part-part-whole problems" (e.g., "There are 4 children in a room. Two are girls. How many are boys?")
- "Compare problems" (e.g., "I have 4 blocks. You have 2 blocks. How many more blocks do I have than you have?")
- "Missing-addend problems" (e.g., "I have 2 books. I need 4 books. How many more books do I need to get?")

Although the five examples given of these types of subtraction problems are different, they all can be represented mathematically in the same way. For instance, to compare 4 and 2 (see fig. 2.1), once you see the twos in each number (shown as pairs), finding how much more 4 is than 2 represents the same action as removing 2 (or one pair) from the set of 4 (or two pairs). In other words, to find the answer to a comparing question, you can use a separating action. Similarly, with a part-part-whole situation, if you think of 2 as one part of 4, to find the other part, you would remove (or separate) the known part from the whole. Missing-addend situations can be modeled similarly.

Fig. **2.1.**

Representation of comparing 4 and 2 by identifying pairs of 2

It is essential that these different types of subtraction situations be presented to primary school students to ensure their familiarity with all of them, since research shows that students don't see the relationships among them. The part-part-whole method has been particularly effective in showing the intrinsic relationship between addition and subtraction. Joining the two parts gives us the whole, and if we know one part and the whole, subtracting gives us the other part.

The activities Frumps' Fashions, Frames, and Park Your Car all present addition and subtraction situations for students to consider. In Frumps' Fashions, the focus is on the language of addition (e.g., *join, altogether, total, in all*) and of subtraction (e.g., *how many are left? how many more?*). The main actions emphasized in the stories that form the basis for the activity are *joining* (leading to addition sentences) and *separating* or *comparing* (leading to subtraction sentences).

Frames focuses students on organizing their work with addition and subtraction through the use of five- and ten-frames. These frames help students think of other numbers in relation to 5 or 10—for example, they can think of 8 as either 3 more than 5 (5 + 3) or as 2 less than 10 (10 – 2). See figure 2.2.

Fig. **2.2.**

A ten-frame arrangement for 8

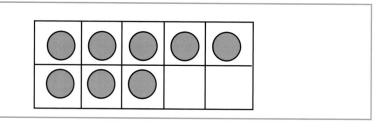

After becoming comfortable with arrangements of chips in these frames, students solve simple addition and subtraction problems by using the frames. The activity emphasizes the number facts strategy "make a 10." It encourages the use of number sentences with the symbols for addition and subtraction.

In Park Your Car, students begin with a parking lot that is essentially a ten-frame, and then they park and "unpark" small toy cars. They play a game in which the number on a rolled die indicates the number of cars coming into the parking lot or leaving it at a particular time. The students explore questions that turn on addition as well as several different meanings of subtraction. These include "separating" questions that can be answered by subtracting (for example, "How many are left?" "If the total is 6 and 2 leave, how many are there now?") and "comparing" questions that can be answered either by subtracting or by thinking of missing addends ("How many more?" "How many fewer?" "How many are needed?").

Multiplication and Division

The next operations that students encounter are multiplication and division. At this level, students do not need formal symbols for these operations. Rather, they should focus on the actions that underlie the operations so that when they meet these operations more formally later, they will be building on prior experience.

Students develop the concept of multiplication through the joining of numbers of equal-sized groups. Later, in higher grades, students extend their understanding of multiplication through the use of arrays, area, and combination models. In the activity Mirror Multiplication, students use mirrors to produce an image of a set of objects, and they treat the image as a second, equal-sized group. Thus, if four objects sit in front of the mirror, the viewer sees two groups of four—the real objects and their images. By hinging mirrors, students can see even more images of the original objects, investigating three, four, or more groups of equal size.

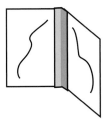

Division arises in a number of types of situations, including sharing, finding how many sets of equal size are in a larger set, and determining fractional relationships. However, the focus in this book is on division as sharing (Carpenter, Carey, and Kouba 1990). In Jamal's Balloons, students use counters to represent balloons and plates to represent different people who are sharing the balloons. No symbols are required. Initially, you might restrict the division situation to sharing. (For example, if there are 6 balloons and 3 children share them, each child gets 2, so there are 3 sets of 2). Afterward, you might want to introduce your students to division as repeated subtraction. (If there are 6 balloons and 3 children share them, each child can take one balloon, subtracting 3 repeatedly from the total number of balloons, until the children have distributed all the balloons.)

See "An Alternative to Basic-Skills Remediation" (Hankes 1996) on the CD-ROM for more detail about the different types of word problems and children's solution strategies.

Expectations for Students' Accomplishment

By the end of grade 2, students should be able to use numbers and symbols to represent addition and subtraction situations, act out addition and subtraction stories with concrete materials, write equations to

See "Helping at Home" (Kline 1999) on the CD-ROM for ideas for simple games for home and the classroom to support mathematical understanding.

describe problems, and write story problems to go with equations. Students should also be able to represent specific situations that involve joining equal-sized groups or sharing a total to make equal-sized groups as a foundation for later work in multiplication and division. Students' understanding of the addition and subtraction operations is necessary for them to succeed in mathematics beyond grade 2.

Frumps' Fashions

Prekindergarten–Kindergarten

Summary

Students learn the meaning and language of addition as they use chips to represent objects in stories and join groups of objects to tell how many *in all* or *altogether*. The same story approach is used to introduce students to subtraction. They compare groups of objects to tell *how many more*. They remove a subset of objects to tell *how many are left*. They learn to "write" the problems that stories pose by recording addition and subtraction number sentences, and they learn to tell stories for number sentences presented to them.

Goals

- Use chips to represent objects
- Explore addition as the joining of groups
- Use + and = to write addition number sentences
- Use – and = to write subtraction number sentences
- Learn the language of addition (*in all*, *altogether*) and of subtraction (*how many more? how many are left?*)

Prior Knowledge

- Counting up to ten objects
- Recognizing the numerals 0 through 10
- Writing the numerals 0 through 10

Materials

- Ten chips for each student and ten for classroom demonstration
- A work mat (a piece of construction paper with a line down the center from top to bottom on one side) for each student and one for classroom demonstration

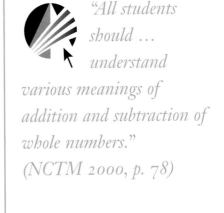

"All students should … understand various meanings of addition and subtraction of whole numbers."
(NCTM 2000, p. 78)

Activity

Conduct the activity with the whole class. Seat students in a semicircle facing you and the chalkboard.

Engage

Give each student a work mat and ten chips, and take the same materials for yourself. Use the blank side of the work mat. Read aloud the first story, "Mrs. Frump's Hats." As you name each hat, place a chip on your work mat to represent it, and have the students do the same on their work mats. Check to be sure that students are following directions.

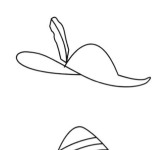

Mrs. Frump's Hats

Mrs. Frump loves hats. She loves to wear hats to parties.

"How many hats do I have in all?" Mrs. Frump wonders.

Let's help Mrs. Frump figure out how many hats she has altogether.

Mrs. Frump has a green hat with a feather.

[Pause. Put one chip on your mat to stand for the green hat with a feather.]

Mrs. Frump has a blue hat with stripes.

[Pause. Put one chip on your work mat to stand for the blue hat with stripes.]

Mrs. Frump has a red hat with stars.

[Pause. Put one chip on your work mat to stand for the red hat with stars.]

Mrs. Frump has a yellow hat with balloons.

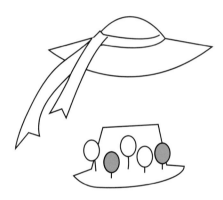

[Pause. Put one chip on your work mat to stand for the yellow hat with balloons.]

Mrs. Frump has a turquoise hat with ribbons.

[Pause. Put one chip on your work mat to stand for the turquoise hat with ribbons.]

How many hats does Mrs. Frump have altogether?

[Pause.]

Count the chips, or let your students count them, to tell how many hats Mrs. Frump has in all. (5)

Explore

Have students turn over their work mats to the side with the line drawn down the center. For the following stories, students will use chips to represent objects in two groups, each with one or more objects. They will show a group on each side of the line.

As you read the next story, "Mr. Frump's Bow Ties," show your students where to place chips and how many chips to place. You should model the groups on your mat as you read aloud.

Mr. Frump's Bow Ties

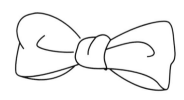

Mr. Frump loves bow ties. He loves to wear bow ties to parties with Mrs. Frump.

"How many bow ties do I have in all?" Mr. Frump wonders.

Let's help Mr. Frump figure out how many bow ties he has altogether.

Mr. Frump has two purple bow ties.

[Put down two chips on one side of the line to show the purple bow ties.]

Mr. Frump has four brown bow ties.

[Put down four chips on the other side of the line to show the brown bow ties.]

How many bow ties does Mr. Frump have in all?

How can we figure it out? *[Wait for a suggestion.]*

When a student comes up with the idea of merging, or combining, the two groups, say, "Good. Let's push the two groups of chips together. Now count the chips to tell the number of bow ties in all." (6)

Next, read the two stories that follow, but give no directions for the placement of chips, and do not model the groups. Pause after each group is described to give students enough time to use their chips to represent the objects.

Watch to see if your students can place the chips on their own.

Mrs. Frump's T-Shirts

Mrs. Frump loves T-shirts. She loves to wear T-shirts when she gardens.

"How many T-shirts do I have in all?" Mrs. Frump wonders.

Can you help Mrs. Frump figure out how many T-shirts she has altogether?

Mrs. Frump has five T-shirts with pictures of bumblebees.

[*Pause*]

Mrs. Frump has three T-shirts with pictures of flowers.

[*Pause*]

How many T-shirts does Mrs. Frump have altogether? (8)

You may want to check your students' work and perhaps go through the problem with them before reading the next story. See if they place the chips with greater confidence as you read "Mrs. Frump's Pants."

Mrs. Frump's Pants

Mrs. Frump loves pants. She loves to wear pants with T-shirts when she gardens.

"How many pairs of pants do I have in all?" Mrs. Frump wonders.

Can you help Mrs. Frump figure out how many pairs of pants she has altogether?

Mrs. Frump has three pairs of plaid pants.

[*Pause*]

Mrs. Frump has six pairs of red pants.

[*Pause*]

How many pairs of pants does Mrs. Frump have in all? (9)

At a later time, help your students understand subtraction in a similar manner. Subtracting as "comparing" is the focus of "Mr. Frump's Belts." Subtracting as "taking away" or "giving away" is the focus of "Mr. Frump's Pajamas." Model the subtraction stories along with the students. Tell them to use the side of the work mat with the line.

Mr. Frump's Belts

Mr. Frump loves belts. He loves to wear belts when he gardens with Mrs. Frump.

Mr. Frump has two different colors of belts. He has yellow belts and green belts.

"Do I have more yellow belts or green belts?" Mr. Frump wonders.

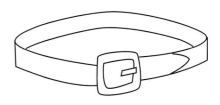

Let's help Mr. Frump answer this question.

We know Mr. Frump has two different colors of belts.

Mr. Frump has four green belts.

[*Pause. Put the chips on one side of the line to show the number of green belts.*]

Mr. Frump has six yellow belts.

[*Pause. Put the chips on the other side of the line to show the number of yellow belts.*]

Does Mr. Frump have more green belts or more yellow belts? (yellow)

How many more does he have? (2)

How do you know?

For the next story, "Mr. Frump's Pajamas" tell the students to use the unlined side of the work mat.

Mr. Frump's Pajamas

Mr. Frump loves bright red pajamas. He always sleeps well in bright red pajamas.

Mr. Frump has ten pairs of bright red pajamas.

[*Pause. Put down ten chips to show Mr. Frumps ten pairs of bright red pajamas.*]

Mrs. Frump can't sleep. She tosses and turns all night.

Mr. Frump gives Mrs. Frump six pairs of his bright red pajamas to help her sleep.

[*Pause. Take away six chips to show the number of pairs of bright red pajamas that Mr. Frump gives to Mrs. Frump.*]

How many bright red pajamas does Mr. Frump have left? (4)

Be sure to include addition sentences in which the first or second addend is zero (e.g., $0 + 3 = 3$; $4 + 0 = 4$) and subtraction sentences in which zero is subtracted ($5 - 0 = 5$) or the answer is zero ($4 - 4 = 0$).

Extend

Tell students that you will show them a way to "write" the problems about the Frumps' clothes with numbers and symbols. Retell the addition stories about bow ties, T-shirts, and pants. As you tell each story, record the corresponding addition sentence. For example, for "Mr. Frump's Bow Ties," write $2 + 4 = 6$.

Call on students to tell what the 2, 4, and 6 represent. (The 2 is the number of purple bow ties, the 4 is the number of brown bow ties, and the 6 is the number of bow ties altogether.) Tell the students that they can think of the "+" as saying "push the groups of chips together." The "=" means that 6 is another name for $2 + 4$.

After the students have helped you write the story problems with addition sentences, you may want to record other addition sentences on the board and have students create stories to match the sentences.

Later, when the children have modeled the subtraction stories with chips, show them how to write the story problems using numbers and symbols. Again, you can write other subtraction sentences on the board and let your students create stories to match them.

Discussion

Students may be at varying levels of development in their abilities to follow the actions of the stories and accurately represent the number of objects in each group. For students who are experiencing difficulty, you may want to devote greater time to presenting more stories of the type depicted in the "Explore" section of this activity. You could also make audiotapes of story problems for students to listen to and model on their own.

If your students have difficulty in understanding the addition and subtraction number sentences, you may need to model and explain more of these sentences before the students are able to write them. If your students quickly grasp the ideas behind addition and subtraction number sentences, you may want to have them write their own story problems and the corresponding number sentences.

Frumps' Fashions not only develops students' understanding of the meanings of addition and subtraction but also is a powerful vehicle for enhancing literacy skills, particularly listening and storytelling skills.

p. 91

Frames

Prekindergarten–Kindergarten

Summary

Students are introduced to addition and subtraction on five- and ten-frames. They figure out the number of chips they must add or take away from a frame to produce a specific number.

Goals

* Add and subtract (numbers to 10)
* Learn the language of addition (*in all, altogether*) and subtraction (*take away, are left, how many more?*)

Prior Knowledge

* Counting up to ten objects
* Knowing the language of comparison: *more, less, fewer*

Materials

* A copy of the blackline master "Frames" for each student
* Ten chips (or other counters) for each student

Activity

Engage

Give a copy of the blackline master "Frames" to each student, along with five chips (or other counters). Call on a student to count the number of squares in the five-frame. Point out that the frame's name refers to the number of squares. Have students take three chips and place them in the frame, one chip in a square. Any arrangement of the chips is acceptable. Point out that the chips will be easier to count if they are placed in the squares beginning at the left. See figure 2.3 to illustrate the number 3. Then have students use the five-frame and their chips to show the numbers 1, 2, 4, and 5.

Fig. **2.3.**

Five-frame arrangements for the number 3

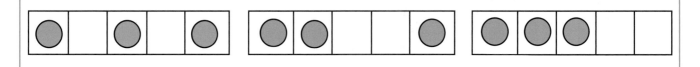

Give each student another five chips, for a total of ten. Have the students look now at the ten-frame on the blackline master. Ask, "How is the ten-frame like the five-frame?" (The ten-frame is like two five-frames, one above the other.) Tell the students to show the number 6, filling the first row (the top row) and then beginning to fill the next row, from left to right. Call on students to show 7, 8, and 9. (See figure 2.4.) Finally, have a student show 10.

Read to the students from a counting book that explores the numbers 1–10 in order, such as *Fish Eyes: A Book You Can Count On* by Lois

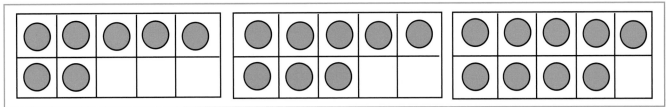

Fig. **2.4.**

The numbers 7, 8, and 9 represented on a ten-frame

Ehlert (2001). As you read about each number, have students use their ten-frames and chips to show that number.

Explore

Have students place a specific number of chips on the ten-frame. Ask them to describe their frames. (See figure 2.5.)

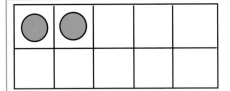 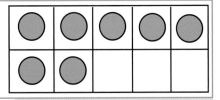

Fig. **2.5.**

Chips on students' ten-frames

In describing the last arrangement in figure 2.5, students might note: "The number is two more than five," "It is three more than four," "It has three empty spaces," "You need three more to get ten," or "It's three less than ten."

Have students display a certain number of chips—for example, four chips—on their ten-frames. Ask the following questions, and have students check by placing or removing chips:

- "Imagine that you have one more chip. How many chips would you have altogether?"

Repeat for two more, one less, and two less.

- "How many chips will you have to put on your frame to have seven chips in all? Nine chips in all? Ten chips in all?"

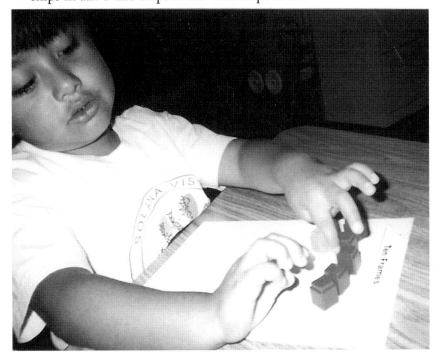

- "How many chips will you have to take away from your frame so that you have one chip left? Zero chips left?"

Extend

Show your students how to record their work with number sentences. Have the students show four chips on their ten-frames. Ask them to place one more chip on the frame and tell you the total number of chips. Record 4 + 1 = 5 on the chalkboard.

Initially, focus only on addition sentences. Call on students to tell what each number in the expression means—that the 4 is the number of chips on the frame at the start, the 1 is the chip that is added, and the 5 is the total number of chips. Point out that the symbol "+" tells us to add the 1 to the 4 and that the "=" tells us that the 5 "is another name for" 4 + 1.

Repeat this process with other sums. Some students may be able to tell you how to record the number sentences. Others may be able to record the sentences themselves.

After several weeks of addition sentence experience, you may want to begin recording subtraction sentences. Point out that in this activity "–" (minus) means to take away.

Discussion

In Frames, the conventional method of placing chips, left to right and beginning with the first (top) row, helps students relate certain arrangements of chips with specific numbers and develops mental images of those arrangements. They "see" pairs of addends that sum to particular numbers. For example, students see the number 7 as the sum 5 + 2 (5 chips in the top row and 2 in the bottom row), 8 as the sum 5 + 3, and so on. These mathematical images of the sums will benefit students as they advance in their understanding of addition.

The Frames activity introduces students to two meanings of subtraction: removing (taking away) a subset and determining how many more are needed. Using the second meaning, students see the number of empty squares in a ten-frame as the "number of additional chips needed" to make 10. For example, a ten-frame with seven squares filled could model the problem, "I have 7 pencils. How many more do I need to make 10?"

Students can continue to use the ideas and skills that they mastered in this activity by working with the applet Frames on the CD-ROM.

Park Your Car

Grades 1–2

Summary

Students explore addition and subtraction by "parking" and removing toy cars from parking lots that each hold ten cars. They then create and model stories about cars entering and leaving the lot. The activity allows them to explore different models of subtraction, including finding a missing addend, taking away, and comparing.

Goals

- Understand various meanings of the addition and subtraction of whole numbers
- Recognize the inverse relationship between the operations addition and subtraction
- Understand the effects of adding and subtracting whole numbers
- Gain familiarity with the language of addition (*in all*, *altogether*, and *total*) and subtraction (*take away*, *what is left? how many more?*)
- Write number sentences to solve problems

Prior Knowledge

- Counting sets of objects

Materials

- Twenty small toy cars, or twenty chips to represent cars, for each pair of students
- A copy of the blackline master "One Parking Lot" for each student
- A copy of the blackline master "Two Parking Lots" for each pair of students
- A number cube (numbered 1–6) for each pair of students

Activity

Engage

Pair up your students, and give each pair one number cube, two copies of the blackline master "One Parking Lot," and twenty small toy cars or chips. Tell the students that they will be using these materials to play a game, "Park Your Car," about a parking lot.

Describe the parking-lot game to the students. The goal of the game is to be the first person in each pair to fill the parking lot. Students roll the cube to determine who plays first. The student who rolls the higher number begins. The students then take turns rolling the cube and placing corresponding numbers of small cars in their own parking lots. Each student can fill the lot only by rolling the number that tells exactly how many cars the student needs to fill it. For example, if a student has seven cars on her lot and rolls a 5, she cannot park any cars because five more cars won't fit in her lot. The

pp. 92, 93

student then loses a turn and waits for another turn to roll a 3 or less. Have the students play the parking lot game several times.

Explore

Tell stories about cars in parking lots. Have students use their cars (or chips) and parking lots to model and solve the following story problems about one parking lot:

- Sam's lot has 4 cars. How many more cars have to park in Sam's parking lot so that it is full?
- Shonda's parking lot has 6 cars parked in it. Three cars drive out. Five cars drive in. How many cars are now in Shonda's parking lot?
- Jeremy's parking lot has 7 cars in it. Ann Marie's parking lot has 9 cars in it. How many more cars are in Ann Marie's lot than in Jeremy's lot?
- Sue's parking lot has 5 cars in it. A few minutes ago, her parking lot had 8 cars in it. How many cars left Sue's parking lot?

As you create additional stories about parking lots, be sure to include a variety of types of addition and subtraction problems. You should include problems that involve missing addends, taking away, and comparing. You might want to choose different students to use a parking lot on the overhead projector and demonstrate the solutions to the stories.

After going over a few story problems, choose students to be the leaders who will create story problems for their classmates to solve. Students' stories may be very complex, and the problems that they pose may be very challenging for their classmates. This practice is excellent!

Extend

After students are comfortable with parking-lot stories that ask them to add and subtract numbers up to 10, distribute a copy of the blackline master "Two Parking Lots" to each pair of students. Have students work together to solve the following story problems about greater numbers of cars in two parking lots:

- Dan has 2 parking lots. He has 8 cars in one and 9 in the other. How many cars does he have altogether?

- George has 8 cars in one lot and 7 cars in another parking lot. Five more cars need to park. Does George have room for them all?

- Gina has a "Lot Full" sign on both of her parking lots. Three cars leave one parking lot. Then 5 cars leave the other parking lot. Four cars are lined up waiting to park. After these cars park, how many more cars can Gina park before she has to put up the "Lot Full" sign again?

For students who are successful with these story problems, you may wish to design larger parking lots and introduce problems that involve two-digit addition and subtraction.

Discussion

Young students should develop an understanding of the various meanings of subtraction. In the story problems about parking lots, students use subtraction to solve "take away" problems ("I had 5 cars, and 3 drove away. How many are left?"); comparison problems ("I have 7 cars and you have 3. How many more cars do I have than you?"); and missing-addend problems ("I have 8 cars. How many more cars must arrive before my lot is full?"). Stories like these and the addition stories about cars entering and leaving the parking lots increase students' understanding of the inverse relationship between addition and subtraction.

The parking lots in this activity are also designed to strengthen students' use of 10 as a guidepost in solving addition and subtraction exercises. For example, when the students are finding the sum of 8 and 9 using the two parking lots, they should realize that they can use 10 as a marker. They might think, "Nine is just 1 less than 10, so 8 + 9 must be 1 less than 8 + 10, which I know is 18, so the answer must be 17." Or they might think, "Eight is 2 less than 10, and 9 is 1 less than 10, so 8 + 9 must be 3 less than 20." Another student might reason, "Eight is 2 away from 10, so if I add 2 to 8 to make 10, I should take 2 away from 9. Then I can add the 10 and the 7." To discover what methods students are employing, encourage them to describe the strategies that they use to solve these problems.

*"Students learn basic number combinations and develop strategies for computing that make sense to them when they solve problems with interesting and challenging contexts. Through class discussions, they can compare the ease of use and ease of explanation of various strategies."
(NCTM 2000, p. 84)*

Jamal's Balloons

Grades K–1

Summary

Students use paper plates and chips or other counters to dramatize division story problems. These activities show division as making equal groups. Students also explore division with remainders.

Goal

- Share by making equal groups and counting the number in each group

Prior Knowledge

- Knowing basic addition facts

Materials

- Twelve chips for each student and twelve for classroom demonstration
- Six paper plates for each student
- Poster board and tape (or felt board, if available)
- Six pictures of children, three boys and three girls
- Overhead projector or chalkboard

Activity

Engage

Display a blank poster board lengthwise so that all your students can see it. Show the students a picture of a boy (drawn or cut from a magazine). Begin the story:

Jamal's Balloons

There is a boy is named Jamal.

[Tape the picture at the bottom of the poster board.]

Jamal has twelve balloons.

[Show the students twelve chips.]

Let's pretend that these chips are Jamal's balloons.

[Tape the chips in a row above the picture of Jamal.]

What could we do with the chips to show that all the balloons are Jamal's?

[Wait until a student suggests grouping the chips together in a bunch, and then move them close together above Jamal.]

Jamal's best friend is Orpheo.

[Tape a picture of a second boy at the bottom of the poster board.]

Orpheo says, "Hi, Jamal! Wow! Look at all the balloons!"

Students may need to deal out the twelve chips one at a time to the people who are sharing the balloons in the stories, perhaps saying, "One for you, one for you, …," until they have distributed the balloons evenly.

Jamal wants to share the balloons with Orpheo. He wants Orpheo and himself to have the same number of balloons after sharing.

How many balloons should Jamal give to Orpheo? How many balloons will each boy have then?

[Let a student help you move the chips, using new tape if necessary, to show six chips above Orpheo and six chips above Jamal.]

Jamal and Orpheo have a friend named Melissa.

[Tape a picture of a girl at the bottom of the poster board beside Jamal and Orpheo.]

Melissa says, "Hi, Jamal! Hi, Orpheo! Gee, what pretty balloons!" Jamal and Orpheo want to share the balloons with Melissa. They want everyone to have the same number of balloons after sharing.

How many balloons should Jamal and Orpheo each give to Melissa? How many balloons will each child have then?

[Let students describe how to share the balloons, and then let a student help you move the chips to show four balloons above each pictured child.]

Jamal, Orpheo, and Melissa also have a friend named Nara.

[Tape a picture of a second girl at the bottom of the poster board beside Jamal, Orpheo, and Melissa.]

Nara says, "Hi, Jamal! Hi, Orpheo! Hi, Melissa! Wow, you all have balloons!"

Jamal, Orpheo, and Melissa want to share the balloons with Nara. They want everyone to have the same number of balloons after sharing.

"The strategies used to solve such problems—the repeated joining of, and partitioning into, equal subgroups—thus become closely associated with the meaning of multiplication and division, respectively." (NCTM 2000, p. 84)

How many balloons should Jamal, Orpheo, and Melissa each give to Nara? How many balloons will each child have then?

[Again, let students describe how to share the balloons, and then let a student help you move the chips to show three balloons above each pictured child.]

Jamal, Orpheo, Melissa, and Nara play with the balloons all afternoon.

Explore

Arrange the students in groups of four. Give each group six plates and twelve chips. Write or sketch the five problem situations below, one at a time, on overhead transparencies or the chalkboard:

- Four children want to share 8 balloons.
- Three children want to share 12 balloons.
- Two children want to share 12 balloons.
- Six children want to share 12 balloons.
- Two children want to share 10 balloons.

Tell the students that their plates stand for children and their chips stand for balloons. Explain that they should help the children in each situation share the balloons equally. After students have an opportunity to consider each problem, ask them to tell how many balloons each child has and how they found the answer.

Extend

You can extend this activity by helping students figure out what to do if the number of items does not divide evenly among the children. Begin with a picture of three children and seven chips to represent cookies. Tell the students that the three children want to share the cookies, with each getting the same number. Have the students decide where to move the counters. When they have given two chips to each child, ask, "What should I do with this chip, or cookie, that is left?"

Students will probably make a variety of suggestions, including giving away the extra cookie or cutting it into pieces. Take time to discuss these alternatives, and talk about situations in which each alternative would be appropriate. (If the extra item is a balloon, you can't cut it up without destroying it. If the extra is a cookie, as here, you just might cut it into equal pieces.) Repeat the scenario, with the three children sharing several other quantities. Some of the problems should have remainders, and some should not.

Discussion

Most K–1 students have an intuitive understanding of division as sharing. In their everyday lives, they encounter many situations in which items are left over after being shared equally. The process in the "Extend" section can help students understand different ways to deal with this type of situation.

You may want to have children verify the results of the sharing by using repeated addition. For example, if three children share twelve balloons and each gets four balloons, then the solution can be checked by adding 4 + 4 + 4. Likewise, if three children share thirteen balloons, then each gets four, with one left over: 4 + 4 + 4 + 1 = 13.

Mirror Multiplication

Grade 2

Summary

Students use pairs of mirrors to create reflected images and model multiplication. They record their actions by describing numbers of groups and the number in each group.

Goals

- Identify equal groups in multiplication
- Record multiplication according to the number of groups, the number in each group, and the total
- Recognize that reflections duplicate the items being reflected

Prior Knowledge

- Adding small numbers
- Counting by twos, threes, and fours

Materials

- Unbreakable rectangular mirrors, all the same size, one for each student
- Six chips for each student
- Masking tape for each pair of students to hinge two mirrors together

Activity

Engage

Give each student a mirror and three chips. Have the students place three chips in front of their mirrors. Ask them what they see (two groups of three chips—the three real chips and the three chips forming their reflected image) and have them give the total number of chips (both real and reflected) that they see. Write—

2 groups of 3 are 6.

Let pairs of children place different numbers of chips in front of their mirrors, each time counting the total number of chips that they see. After each experiment, have them write—

2 groups of ___ are ___.

Ask students to share their results. List them all on the chalkboard in ascending order:

2 groups of 1 are 2
2 groups of 2 are 4
2 groups of 3 are 6
.
.
.
2 groups of 6 are 12

"*All students should … understand situations that entail multiplication and division, such as equal groupings of objects and sharing equally.*" (NCTM 2000, p. 78)

"*All students should … recognize and apply … flips.*" (NCTM 2000, p. 96)

To create the hinged mirrors, tape together two mirrors along edges of equal length. Be sure that there is enough slack to fold the mirrors closer together or open them wider.

Help students observe how the total numbers increase by 2. Talk about why this happens. (Every time a real counter is placed in front of the mirror, it has a reflected image, so we see two counters.)

Explore

Help your students use tape to hinge pairs of mirrors together. (Alternatively, prepare sets of hinged mirrors in advance.) Have the students first fold the mirrors so that they are not touching but are angled enough to be freestanding. (See figure 2.6.) Then place two chips inside the space between the mirrors. Ask the students what they observe. All students should see multiple groups of two counters, but some will see more groups than others, depending on how close together their mirrors are. Have the students change the space between the mirrors so that they can see that it is possible to see more and more sets of two as the mirrors get closer and closer together.

Fig. **2.6.**

Hinged mirror showing multiple groups of chips

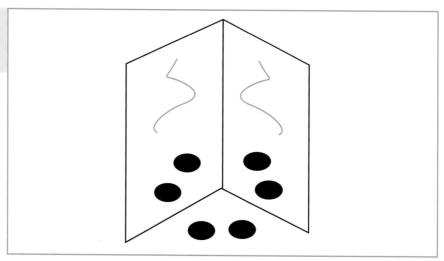

Assign each pair of students a number between 2 and 6, and tell them to place that many chips between their hinged mirrors. Have each pair change the space between the mirrors so that they can see different numbers of copies (reflected images) of their chips. One student should be responsible for holding the mirror while the other student counts; they can switch roles each time they move the mirror. Once the students see a different grouping, they should record the number of groups and count the total number of visible chips, both actual ones and reflected images. For example, the students' work might be as follows:

3 groups of 3 are 9
4 groups of 3 are 12
5 groups of 3 are 15
:
:

Encourage your students to talk about numbers that come up in more than one situation. For example, the number 12 results from 4 groups of 3, 3 groups of 4, and 6 groups of 2.

Extend

Ask your students to use their chips and mirrors to figure out all the different ways to find various totals. For example, if they want to see a

Chapter 3 in *Navigating through Geometry in Prekindergarten– Grade 2* (Findell et al. 2001) explores symmetry and reflections. Students use one mirror in Mirror Pictures to explore mirror reflections. They use a mirror or a colored plastic device called a Mira to identify one or more lines of symmetry.

total of twelve chips, they might choose to put four chips down and adjust the mirror until they can see three groups of four. Some students might like to experiment with more mirrors or even analyze and construct simple kaleidoscopes. This work would make an excellent connection with science.

Discussion

The effects of hinging mirrors is always surprising and interesting to students. This unique approach to creating multiple copies of a group is an inviting way to introduce multiplication. Some teachers may wish to introduce the "×" symbol and represent three groups of two as 3×2. However, the emphasis at this age should be on having students represent multiplication with oral or written descriptions (for example, 3 groups of 2) or with their own notation, including diagrams. You should not expect that students will memorize any of the multiplication facts at this time but will simply become familiar with the concept of multiplication and with which numbers come up in which situations.

Conclusion

This chapter has introduced students to the meanings of the four basic operations—addition, subtraction, multiplication, and division. Chapter 3 expands ideas about addition and subtraction to include basic fact strategies, estimation, and computation.

NAVIGATING *through* NUMBER *and* OPERATIONS

Chapter 3
Fact Strategies, Estimation, and Computation

In kindergarten through grade 2, students build their addition and subtraction skills first by learning basic addition and subtraction facts and then by developing their ability to estimate and calculate sums and differences involving two-digit numbers.

Because a knowledge of basic facts is a crucial building block, teachers need to spend time ensuring that students learn these facts. Eventually, students should memorize them, but not until they have had considerable experience with the facts in many situations. Although addition and subtraction facts are sometimes taught separately, there is a value in considering facts about both operations at the same time. Since every subtraction fact can be rewritten as an addition fact (e.g., $14 - 8 = \square$ can be rewritten as $8 + \square = 14$), it makes sense to think of subtraction along with addition.

Initially, students learn that $5 + 3$ is 8 by counting out five objects, then three more, and finally counting all eight objects, saying, "1, 2, 3, 4, 5, 6, 7, 8." This strategy is called "counting all." According to Ginsburg, Klein, and Starkey (1998), most six-to-seven-year-olds then realize that it is more efficient to start at 5 and say, "6, 7, 8." This strategy is called "counting on." Many researchers (Fuson 1992) make a distinction between students who count on from the first number and those who always count on from the greater number. Students who find $3 + 8$ by counting on from 8 and saying "9, 10, 11," are working more efficiently than those who count on from 3 and say, "4, 5, 6, 7, 8, 9, 10, 11."

There are a number of other helpful strategies that students can employ to use a known fact to help them learn one that is not already known. Examples of some of these strategies follow:

"Children move through a progression of different procedures to find the sum of single-digit numbers.... First, children count out objects for the first addend, count out objects for the second addend, and count all of the objects (count all). This general counting-all procedure then becomes abbreviated, internalized, and abstracted as children ... notice that they do not have to count the objects for the first addend but can start with the number in the first or the larger addend and count on the objects in the other addend (count on)."
(Mathematics Learning Study Committee 2001, pp. 187–88)

- "Finding a double"—converting an unknown fact like 5 + 7 into a known double, such as 6 + 6. According to Carpenter and Moser (1984), doubles are among the easiest facts for students to learn.
- "Finding a near-double"—recognizing 8 + 7 as one more than the double 7 + 7 or one less than the double 8 + 8.
- "Making a 10"—thinking of 7 + 8 as 7 + (3 + 5), which equals (7 + 3) + 5, or 10 + 5, or 15.

Many teachers use 10 as a benchmark, or guidepost, and help students think of how other numbers that are more or less than 10 can be related to 10.

As we have described, students often learn subtraction facts in relation to the appropriate addition fact. Sometimes they use other strategies:
- "Counting up"—finding 12 – 9, for example, by counting up from 9 and keeping track, often on their fingers, of how many numbers they say—"Ten, 11, 12 is three numbers, so 12 – 9 is 3."
- "Counting back"—finding 12 – 9 by counting back from 12 until they say 9 and keeping track, often on their fingers, of how many numbers they say—"Eleven, 10, 9 is three numbers, so the 12 – 9 is 3."
- "Making a 10"—finding 12 – 8 by thinking 12 – 2 is 10, and 10 – 2 gets them down to 8, so they've subtracted 2 and another 2, or 4.

The chapter begins with Double Plus or Minus, which focuses on the strategies of finding doubles and near-doubles. In this activity, students use their knowledge of doubles, sometimes rearranging numbers to make it possible for them to use the near-doubles strategy, particularly with addends 5 through 9. Flip Two offers an excellent opportunity for students to explore "making a 10" as an effective strategy in a game that uses ten-frame cards. Zooey Lunch requires students to use a menu, first to determine total prices and the amount of change, and later to compare prices for different items on the menu. One version of the activity focuses on the use of single-digit numbers, which gives students a chance to practice fact strategies.

The ability to estimate sums and differences is just as important for students to develop as the ability to compute those values. Sometimes, estimation is a vehicle for checking an answer. At other times, an estimate is a sufficient answer on its own. The mental strategies associated with estimation build on the students' knowledge of basic facts (for example, 20 + 30 is 50, since 2 + 3 = 5).

Students practice estimation in Valuable Art and Four in a Row. These activities either explicitly require estimating or help students choose appropriate numbers with which to work. In Valuable Art, students assign price values to different pattern blocks, create designs with the blocks, estimate the numerical values for their designs, and then calculate them. In Four in a Row, students must select which two numbers to add to get a certain total and estimation is very helpful in limiting the possibilities.

In order to develop calculation skills with two-digit numbers, students should be comfortable with place-value concepts. In chapter 1, the activities How Many Ways? and Trading Up or Down reinforced these concepts. The activities in this chapter do not offer instruction in specific procedures for adding or subtracting numbers, but they do encourage students to consider many ways to calculate a sum or difference.

For example, in Valuable Art, students learn that to add six nines, it might be better to add six tens and subtract six. The activities Zooey Lunch, Four in a Row, Make a Match, and Hit the Target all require the students to add and subtract two-digit numbers.

In Zooey Lunch, students total prices, make change, and compare prices on a menu. Four in a Row features a game in which students must determine which pairs of numbers to add from a set of possibilities to allow them to cover up four sums in a row on a game board. At the same time the other team or player will be trying to block the opponent(s) from getting four in a row. In Make a Match, students are given a number and required to decide how many tens and ones to add or take away to match a target number. Some students will use counting strategies, others will use place-value materials, and still others will compute in their heads or on paper to determine how much to add or subtract to reach the target. Hit the Target presents a strategy game that allows students to add a limited set of numbers to a starting number to be first to reach a target number. Part of the strategy is to block the other team from winning.

When students add and subtract numbers, they should consider whether mental operations are more appropriate than paper-and-pencil manipulations. The game in One-Out requires students to add single-digit numbers and two-digit numbers in their heads. Students roll a die (or dice) and keep adding the value rolled to the previous sum until they "freeze" their scores, or until a player rolls a 1, at which time all players lose all points for the round. Mental addition of two-digit and one-digit numbers is important to nurture. For example, to add 26 + 5, students might think, "25 + 5 is 30, and 1 more is 31."

Expectations for Students' Accomplishment

By the end of grade 2, students should be able to determine the sum of two single-digit numbers (basic addition facts) and the difference between two single-digit numbers (the related subtraction facts) by using fact strategies instead of counting. Students should also be able to estimate and calculate sums and differences involving two-digit numbers with and without manipulatives. By the end of second grade, students need efficient strategies for adding and subtracting two-digit numbers. These strategies can be invented methods or traditional algorithms.

introduced to the associative, or grouping, property of addition, realizing, for example, that 6 + (6 + 1) = (6 + 6) + 1. Some students may be ready to encounter parentheses, and this might be a good time to introduce this notation to them. Explain that to find the sum, we use the parentheses to tell us which two numbers to add first.

Flip Two

Grades K–1

Summary

The card game "Flip Two" offers informal practice with sums to 18. Each card shows a number (0 through 9) represented by dots on a ten-frame. In the game, students find the total number of dots on two cards, and then they compare their totals to determine the larger one, which wins the round. The ten-frames encourage the use of the fact strategy "make a 10."

Goals

- Use the fact strategy "make a 10"
- Compose and decompose numbers
- Use basic addition facts with numbers up to 20

Prior Knowledge

- Recognizing numbers in ten-frame formations
- Comparing the numbers 0–18
- Recognizing the numbers 11–18 as 10 and some more

Materials

- One set of the cards on the blackline master "Game Cards for 'Flip Two'" for each student. (You may want to paste the game cards on cardboard and laminate them.)
- Nine small chips for each student

Activity

Engage

Distribute one set of ten game cards and nine chips to each student. Have students find the card that shows nine dots and tell how they know there are nine dots. Encourage them to give a variety of reasons. If students don't suggest that they can see that there is one less than ten dots, ask, "How many more dots do you need to have ten?" "How can this help you to know the number of dots?" Repeat these questions with the card showing seven dots.

Have students pick out the cards with eight dots and four dots. Ask, "How many dots are there in all?" Again, encourage a variety of explanations. Some students may suggest counting all the dots. Other students may suggest counting on from four or eight.

If no one suggests using the "make a 10" strategy, lead your students to it. Say,

- "Suppose we could take some of these four dots and put them on the card with eight dots to make ten."
- "How many of the dots would we need?"
- "How many dots would be left?"
- "How does this help us find the total?"

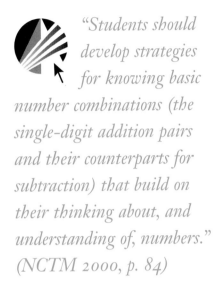

"Students should develop strategies for knowing basic number combinations (the single-digit addition pairs and their counterparts for subtraction) that build on their thinking about, and understanding of, numbers." (NCTM 2000, p. 84)

p. 94

Encourage younger or less advanced students to place four chips on the dots on the card with four dots and model the process.

Repeat the process, first using the cards with nine dots and five dots and then using the cards with eight dots and six dots. Tell the students that this strategy is called "make a 10" and that it is particularly helpful when one of the cards has seven, eight, or nine dots.

Explore

Teach the students how to play "Flip Two." Select four students to model the process. Divide these students into two teams and step them through the rules:

- Two teams of two players pool their game cards, shuffle them, and stack them facedown.

- On each turn, each team flips two cards and finds the total number of dots.

- The teams compare their totals to determine which is greater.

- The team with the greater total wins the round and takes all four cards.

- If both teams have the same total, each team must draw two more cards and add and compare again.

- The team with the greater total this time takes all eight cards.

- The team with the greater number of cards at the end of the game is the winner.

To reinforce the rules of the game, let the four students play several rounds. During the course of play, occasionally ask, "Would this be a good time to use the 'make a 10' strategy?" Demonstrate the strategy both when it would and when it would not be helpful.

Before all the students play on their own, have them summarize the rules. When they clearly understand the rules, organize the students into groups of four, have them pool their cards, and let them play as teams.

Extend

To encourage advanced students to think about the "make a 10" strategy without seeing the actual ten-frames, say, "Suppose you were playing 'Flip Two' and your team turned over cards with nine dots and three dots. How could you use the 'make a 10' strategy to find the total number of dots?" Record the numbers 9 and 3 as you say them. Repeat the process, using different combinations involving at least one 7, 8, or 9. As students become more advanced in their thinking, they can play "Flip Two" with number cards rather than ten-frame dot cards.

Discussion

The "make a 10" strategy is not helpful for students who don't think of the numbers 11 through 18 as being composed of one ten and some ones. These students need to work first on recognizing totals when shown one full ten-frame and one partially full ten-frame. For younger students who have difficulty with this activity, you might want to use the activity Frames that appears in chapter 2 in this book.

pp. 95, 96, 97–98

Zooey Lunch

Grades 1–2

Summary

Students practice adding and subtracting amounts of money. Teachers can adapt the activity to many student levels by simply showing appropriate prices on the menu.

Goals

- Solve problems involving addition and subtraction
- Find values of collections of coins
- Subtract single-digit or two-digit numbers

Prior Knowledge

- Familiarity with the basic coins—penny, nickel, dime, and quarter—and their values
- Ability to add two or more single-digit or two-digit numbers

Materials

- A set of play coins, consisting of ten pennies, five nickels, five dimes, and four quarters, for each pair of students
- A copy of the blackline master "Gorilla's Lunch Menu" for each pair of students
- A copy of the blackline master "How Much?" for each pair of students

Activity

Engage

Present a collection of coins worth less than $1 to students. Call on a student to tell the amount of money represented. For example, you might show four pennies, two dimes, and one quarter to represent 49¢. Tell students that you want to buy something that costs 23¢ and you want to know how much money you will have left. Have a student model a strategy for solving the problem.

Now show 51¢ with a set of coins. Again, tell students that you want to buy something that costs 23¢. Ask, "How much money will be left after I spend 23¢?" This time, ensure that students understand that coin trading may be necessary to answer the question.

Distribute a set of play coins (ten pennies, five nickels, five dimes, and four quarters) to each pair of students. Show two items, one marked with a price of 18¢ and another marked with a price of 34¢. Ask the students—

- "How much do the two items cost altogether?"
- "How much more does the second item cost than the first?"

Explore

Distribute a copy of the blackline master "Gorilla's Lunch Menu A" or "Gorilla's Lunch Menu B" to students, depending on their level. The price list on menu A consists of single-digit prices, and the price list on menu B consists of two-digit prices (see margin). Point out that all the food that Gorilla prepares has an animal theme.

Distribute copies of the blackline master "How Much?" to the students. Questions 5 and 6 ask students to imagine that they have paid for an item with an amount of money that you specify. The questions ask students how much change they would expect to get back. If your students are using price list A, tell them to write in the appropriate box on the blackline master that they have paid 10¢ for each item. If they are using price list B, tell them to write that they have paid $1.00 for each item. Question 9 asks "What two items cost □ together?" If your students are using price list A, have them write 15¢ in the box. If they are using list B, have them write 67¢ in the box.

Have students solve the problems, working in pairs. Encourage them to use their play money if they wish.

Discuss with the students the strategies that they used to solve the problems. Watch particularly for efficient mental strategies—for example, adding 9 and 8 by changing the problem to 10 and 7, or adding 49 and 38 by adding 50 and 38 and subtracting 1. The questions on the blackline master provide practice in adding, subtracting, naming coin values, and problem solving.

Extend

Encourage students to develop their own menus and to create their own problems for other students to solve.

Discussion

One of the strategies that is effective in classes with students of different ability levels or with mixed ages is to use templates that allow numbers to be varied, depending on the ability level of the students. This activity offers one such model; teachers can vary the menu to show new prices by covering those on menu A or B and writing in new numbers.

Students can use any approaches that they find helpful in solving addition and subtraction problems involving amounts of money. Some will actually use the coins, whereas others will use numerical approaches only. Although the standard algorithms or straight recall of facts are appropriate processes for students to use, you should allow your students to use alternative algorithms as well. You should especially encourage efficient approaches for particular situations.

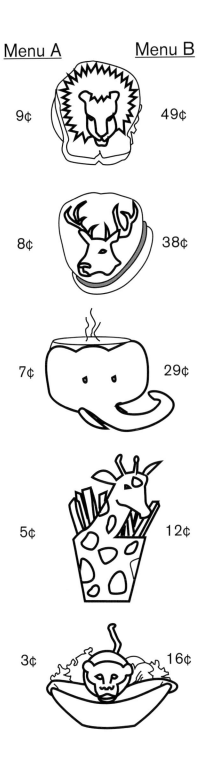

Menu A   Menu B

9¢   49¢

8¢   38¢

7¢   29¢

5¢   12¢

3¢   16¢

A *trapezoid* is a four-sided figure with exactly one pair of parallel sides. A *rhombus* is a four-sided figure with four congruent (same length) sides. (A *square* is a special type of rhombus.) A *regular hexagon* is composed of six equilateral triangles, which can be combined to form three congruent rhombuses or two congruent trapezoids.

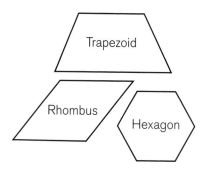

Valuable Art

Grade 2

Summary

The pattern-block triangle is assigned a particular monetary value. Students use that value to assess and compare the values of other pattern blocks and the total costs of several designs created from the pattern blocks.

Goals

- Develop and use strategies for whole-number computation
- Use a variety of methods and tools to compute, including objects, mental computation, estimation, and paper and pencil

Prior Knowledge

- Understanding several meanings of addition and subtraction of whole numbers
- Adding and subtracting one-digit numbers
- Identifying relationships among sizes of pattern blocks

Materials

- Pattern block triangles, trapezoids, rhombuses, and hexagons
- Drawing materials (paper and crayons or colored pencils)
- A copy of the blackline master "Valuable Art" for each student

Activity

Engage

Give each student a collection of pattern blocks (see figure 3.1). Sets of twenty-four green triangles, twelve blue rhombuses, six red trapezoids, and three yellow hexagons will allow students to use whichever shape they prefer to work with to determine the value of the largest design on the blackline master "Valuable Art." Call on students to name the colors and the shapes of the blocks. Because students may not be familiar with the names of the blocks, always refer to them by both their color and mathematical name, as in "red trapezoid." Ask the students to imagine that an art supply store sells tiles the sizes of the pattern blocks and that the cost is based on the size of the tile. Say, "Suppose that today the green triangle is selling for 9¢." Have the students use the green triangle's price to find the value of each of the other pieces.

Encourage the students to use their own techniques for finding these values and to compare their techniques with those of their classmates. For example, one student might say that the hexagon is equal in size to six triangles, so its value must be 54¢. (Explain or illustrate by covering the hexagon with triangles that it takes six triangles to equal one hexagon.) To get 54¢, the student might have reasoned that the triangle is 1¢ less than 10¢, and 6 dimes (10¢ each) is 60¢. And 60¢ – 6¢ is 54¢.

Another student might realize that it takes two triangles to make a rhombus. The rhombus, therefore, must be 9¢ + 9¢, or 18¢. It then takes three rhombuses to make a hexagon, so 18¢ + 18¢ + 18¢ is 54¢. Some students might wish to use paper and pencil or calculators to find these values, whereas others might prefer mental computation.

Explore

After students have found the values of the pattern blocks according to the value of the triangle, tell the students to suppose that the store is having a sale on the tiles. The triangle is now on sale for 4¢. The values of the other tiles are now based on this sale price. Show the students the blackline master entitled "Valuable Art." Ask the students to estimate the cost of filling one of the three designs (reduced here).

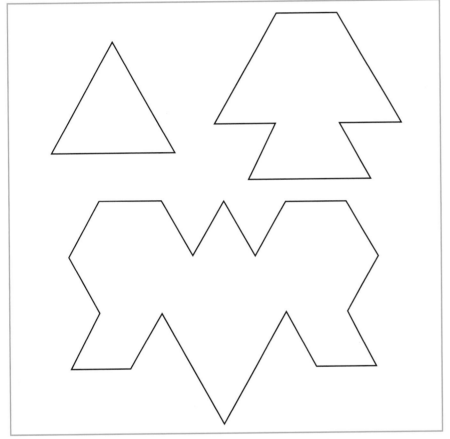

After the students have written down their estimates for the total cost, direct them to use the tiles to cover the design and determine how close their estimates are to the actual cost. Encourage the students to fill their chosen design in different ways. For example, for the largest design, some students might use twenty-four triangles, whereas others might use three hexagons and six triangles. In each example, ask the students to figure out the total cost. Note that each student should find that the total cost of the tiles to fill the largest design is 96¢ regardless of the shapes of the tiles used. (The smallest design is 16¢, and the middle-sized design is 48¢.) Ask the students, "For each design that you chose, did you all use the same blocks to fill it? Did you all get the same total cost for that design? How close were your estimates?" Be sure to call on several students to describe the methods that they used to solve the problem that they chose.

Fig. **3.1.**

Pattern blocks

green

yellow

blue

red

Templates for the appropriate pattern blocks are available on the CD-ROM.

Extend

Have your students use the blocks to create designs of their own, trace around the outside of their designs, and figure out the total cost according to different values for the triangle.

Vary the challenge by assigning a value to one of the pieces and having students make designs with a specific total cost. For example, you might assign the triangle a value of 15¢ and direct students to make a design having a total value of $1.80, or you might assign the hexagon a value of 66¢ and direct students to make a design having a total value of $1.21.

Discussion

This activity combines three strands: number and operations, algebra, and geometry. Students practice mental mathematics, estimation, and the addition of two- and three-digit numbers as they figure out the total cost of filling a design. They use proportional reasoning as they compute the price of one shape on the basis of that of another. They explore geometric relationships as they combine and partition shapes.

When students are computing values of pattern blocks according to the value of a triangle, some students may need to explore the relationships among the sizes of the pieces before computing values. They should find that it takes two triangles to cover the rhombus, three triangles to cover the trapezoid, and six triangles (or three rhombuses or two trapezoids) to cover the hexagon.

When students are computing total costs of designs, they will encounter the need to regroup in the addition of two- and three-digit numbers. Encourage the students to develop their own algorithms for finding these sums, and urge them to explain their methods to one another as they work. It is not necessary to give students formal instruction in the addition algorithms in advance of this activity. Their computational abilities will be more robust and deeply engrained if they struggle to create their own strategies or choose strategies that other students have explained. You may want to use this activity as an opportunity to teach addition with regrouping.

Four in a Row

Grade 2

Summary

Students play a game like tic-tac-toe, in which they estimate sums and add two-digit numbers mentally, with paper and pencil, or with calculators. This two-player game offers practice in finding and estimating sums of two-digit numbers. Players choose two addends from those given, find the sum of the two addends, and write an X or O over that number on the game board. The winner is the first player to get four Xs or Os in a row or a column or on a diagonal.

Goals

- Estimate or mentally compute sums of two-digit numbers
- Practice addition with two-digit numbers
- Develop and communicate game strategies

Prior Knowledge

- Adding two-digit numbers

Materials

- A copy of the blackline master "Game Board for 'Four in a Row'" for each student
- Calculators (optional)
- Twelve chips of one color and twelve chips of another color, one set for each team (optional)
- Paper and pencils

Activity

Engage

Draw a five-square grid on the chalkboard. Tell your students that they're going to play a game like tic-tac-toe but "bigger." Say, "Let's call our new game 'Tic-tic-tac-toe' because now we need to get *four* Xs or Os in a row or a column or on a diagonal." Separate the class into two teams; assign one team to be X and the other to be O. The teams will take turns. Call on a player from each team to come to the board and record his or her team's mark in one cell of the game board. Continue until one team has four marks in a row or until the students recognize that it is no longer possible for either team to do so. Play several games so that the students can become familiar with the game.

To encourage students to think about strategy, ask, "Team O (or X), is there a time in the game when you know your team or the other team will win? How do you know?"

Explore

Give the students copies of the blackline master "Game Board for 'Four in a Row'" (and calculators if you decide to make them available). Tell the students that they are going to play a game like "Tic-tic-tac-

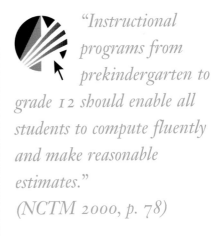

"Instructional programs from prekindergarten to grade 12 should enable all students to compute fluently and make reasonable estimates."
(NCTM 2000, p. 78)

p. 100

toe," except with numbers: "Four in a Row." Teach the students the rules to "Four in a Row." As in "Tic-tic-tac-toe," the winner is the first player to get four Xs or Os in a row or a column or on a diagonal. To place an X or O, the player must choose one number from each number box (A and B), announce the numbers, and find their sum. The player then locates the sum on the game board and marks an X or O in that cell.

Once players have chosen their numbers, they do not have the option of changing their selections. They must announce the sum of their numbers without working with calculators or paper and pencil. These rules encourage students to consider several alternatives first through estimation or mental computation. After players have announced their sums, they should check them on calculators or with pencils and paper. As in "Tic-tic-tac-toe," players may make no more than one mark in any one cell. If a player finds a sum that already has an X or O, her or his turn ends.

Have students play two games, one on each student's copy of the game board. Alternatively, students may use chips to mark the cells; to play again, they simply remove the chips when a game is completed.

After the students have played a couple of games, have them talk about strategies. Ask, "Suppose that you are playing with a new game board that has the number 80. What could you do to help you find a sum of 80?" Students' responses may be general, such as, "I'd find two numbers that add to 80." To probe their thinking, ask such questions as these:

- "How can looking at the tens digits of the addends help?"
- "How can looking at the ones digits of the addends help?"
- "How can rounding numbers help?"
- "How do you add two numbers mentally?"

Extend

To develop your students' skills in estimation and mental computation, draw the number star shown in figure 3.2 on the chalkboard. Ask questions like the following:

- "Which two numbers have a sum greater than 100?" (31, 72), (46, 59), (46, 72), (59, 72) "How do you know? Can you find another pair?"
- "Which two numbers have a sum less than 40?" (5, 16),(5, 31) "How did you decide?"
- "Which two numbers have a sum with a 4 in the ones place?" (5, 59) "How did you decide?"
- "Which two numbers have a sum in the fifties?" (5, 46) "How did you decide?"

Discussion

To gain insight into students' thinking, encourage them to talk about how they are making their decisions. Note whether students' estimates are reasonable and whether they are rounding or focusing on leading digits. Similarly, if students find sums mentally, ask them to share their

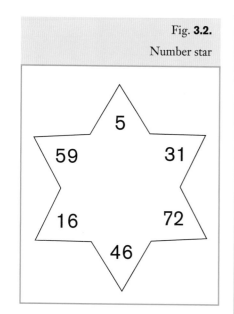

Fig. **3.2.**

Number star

Navigating through Number and Operations in Prekindergarten–Grade 2

strategies. Note whether students focus on the ones digits or add the entire numbers.

Describing their estimation and mental arithmetic techniques helps students clarify and solidify their thinking. Further, through exposure to a variety of techniques, students learn new approaches, which they can choose later to adopt as their own.

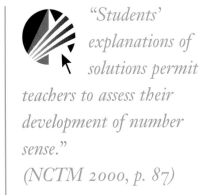

"Students' explanations of solutions permit teachers to assess their development of number sense."
(NCTM 2000, p. 87)

Make a Match

Grades 1–2

Summary

Working in pairs, students decide how many tens and ones to add or subtract to match a target number. Then they record a number sentence to represent their actions.

Goals

- Compose and decompose numbers
- Determine how many tens and ones, as represented with place-value materials, must be added or taken away from a given collection to show a specified number
- Write number sentences to represent actions
- Predict results of adding or taking away tens and ones from a collection of base-ten materials

Prior Knowledge

- Representing and recognizing numbers represented with place-value materials, such as base-ten blocks or Digi-Blocks (ones-blocks and tens-blocks only)
- Reading and writing numerals to 99
- Comparing numbers to 99
- Regrouping tens and ones with concrete materials
- Identifying tens and ones digits in two-digit numbers

Materials

- Place-value materials, such as base-ten blocks or Digi-Blocks, with nine tens and nineteen ones for each pair of students
- Paper and pencils
- Tens and ones place-value materials for the overhead projector (optional)
- Place-value charts for tens and ones (optional)

Note: Use the overhead projector or place-value charts if this is the usual practice in your classroom. No particular tens and ones model is required; use the materials with which your students are most familiar.

Activity

Engage

Display two tens-blocks and five ones-blocks to represent the number 25 (or draw them on the board or show them on a projector). Then write the number 39 on the chalkboard. Call on a student to identify the number, tell whether it is more or less than the number that you just represented with tens and ones, and tell how he or she knows. Repeat a few times, using different tens and ones materials and different

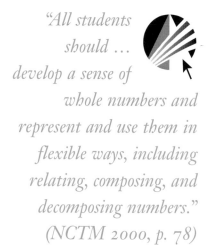

Digi-Blocks™

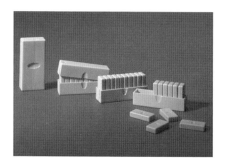

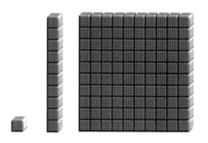

two-digit numbers. Be sure to include numbers that are both greater than and less than the numbers that you have represented with the place-value materials.

Explore

Model the activity with the whole class several times before having the students work on their own in pairs. Distribute nine tens-blocks and nine ones-blocks to pairs of students. The first student uses the place-value materials to represent a two-digit number. The second student chooses a target number, 1 through 99, and writes it on a sheet of paper. This number must differ from the one that the first student represented with the tens and ones materials. Together, the students compare the target number to the number represented by the collection of ten-blocks and one-blocks. If the numbers are the same, the second student should choose another number.

The students then decide whether they need to add to or take away from the collection of tens-blocks and ones-blocks to make the collection match the target number. Encourage the students to tell how they know whether they should add or take away tens-blocks and ones-blocks. After the students have completed the activity several times, have them talk about how they decided on the number of tens-blocks and ones-blocks to add or subtract. Finally, they should record a number sentence to represent their actions.

Invite discussion of their strategies with the following example. Show the number 32 with tens-blocks and ones-blocks. Say, "Suppose the target number is 29. What will you do? Why?"

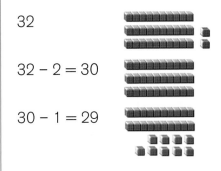

$$32$$
$$32 - 2 = 30$$
$$30 - 1 = 29$$

Note that students may have a variety of ideas. In handling this example, Siobhan, a second-grade student, used a counting strategy. She explained, "You need to get to 29. That's 31, 30, 29." (She held up a finger each time she said a number.), "That's three to take away," she concluded. Her classmate, Nick, said, "Twenty-nine is smaller, so I have to take away. I take two away and I'm at 30. Then I trade to take away one more, for three." Nick modeled these actions with the materials as he described the process.

Emphasize the relationship between the physical actions and the number sentences by asking the following questions about the number sentences:

- "Which number shows the original collection of tens-blocks and ones-blocks?"
- "Which number shows the target number?"
- "Which symbol shows that you added tens and ones?"
- "Which symbol shows that you subtracted tens and ones?"
- "Which number shows how many tens and ones you added?
- "Which number shows how many tens and ones you subtracted?

Extend

As one challenge, students can use the base-ten materials for numbers in the hundreds. They should follow the same process as for two-digit numbers.

As another challenge, students can work without materials. (In this case, you may want to limit them to numbers up to 30.) The students should each record a two-digit number and choose one of them as the

"There are important distinctions between different types of addition and subtraction problems, which are reflected in the way that children think about and solve them." (Carpenter et al. 1999, p. 2)

target number. They then decide how much larger or smaller the other number is compared to the target number. Students may count or use drawings to help them in their work.

Discussion

These "joining" and "separating" models of addition and subtraction with place-value materials involve an initial quantity, a quantity that is joined or separated, and a quantity that results from that action. In the primary grades, students are most often given an initial quantity and a quantity to join to, or separate from, the initial quantity. They then find the result of the joining or separating. These problems are referred to as "result unknown" problems (Carpenter et al. 1999). In Make a Match, students are given initial and result quantities and must figure out the "unknown change" (i.e., addition or subtraction). Working with physical materials helps students develop a visual model for this type of problem, and it increases the likelihood of success later when they confront more abstract "change unknown" problems.

Hit the Target

Grade 2

Summary

Students gain experience in adding, subtracting, and estimating as they compete to be the first to reach a target number. On each turn, students choose to add 1, 2, 5, or 10 to, or subtract it from, the number in play. They analyze the game to determine whether, on a given turn, it is best to add or subtract—and what number should be added or subtracted—to prevent an opponent from reaching the target first.

Goals

- Add 1, 2, 5, or 10 to, or subtract it from, the numbers 1 through 100
- Analyze addition and subtraction options on each turn

Prior Knowledge

- Reading and writing numerals to 100
- Adding and subtracting one- and two-digit numbers
- Knowing basic addition and subtraction facts

Materials

- A calculator (optional)
- A copy of the blackline master "'Hit the Target' Game Sheet" for each pair or each two teams of players

Activity

Engage

Call on a student to choose a starting number from 1 to 90. Record the starting number on the chalkboard. Call on another student to add 10 to that number and give the sum. Record the sum on the chalkboard. Ask a third student to subtract 5 from the sum and give the answer. Record the difference below the previous one. Call on a fourth child to subtract 2 from the previous answer. Record the difference. Continue calling on students to add or subtract 1, 2, 5, or 10 to or from the previous answer and record their answers in the column on the chalkboard.

Explore

Teach your students the game "Hit the Target." This is a game for two players or two teams. Select two students to demonstrate the game. Ask one player to decide on a target number, which must be in the range 50 to 100. Have the other player decide on a starting number, which must be in the range 0 to 30. Tell the players to write these numbers on a game sheet.

The player who chose the target number plays first, adding 1, 2, 5, or 10 to, or subtracting it from, the starting number. Players take turns; each turn consists of the following:

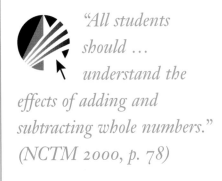

"All students should ... understand the effects of adding and subtracting whole numbers." (NCTM 2000, p. 78)

p. 101

- 1, 2, 5, or 10 is added to or subtracted from the result of the previous computation.
- The new calculation is recorded below the previous answer.

The winner is the player who reaches the target number first. See figure 3.3 for a sample game.

Play the game several times with the entire class before the students play the game on their own. Give a "'Hit the Target' Game Sheet" to each pair or two teams of students. If you decide to have students play in teams, no more than two or three students should be on a team. In that way, students will have several turns within each game.

After all the students have played the game several times, have them talk about how they decided when to add or to subtract as well as how they determined the number to add or subtract.

Ask questions to prompt the students to think more deeply about the game and successive plays. For example, suppose that the target number is 10. You might say to a student, "It's your turn and the last number is 7."

- "What will you do? Why?"
- "If your team adds 1, can the other team win on their next turn?" (Yes. They can add 2.)
- "If your team adds 5, can the other team win on their next turn?" (Yes. They can subtract 2.)
- "If your team adds 10, can the other team win on the next turn?" (No.)

Extend

You can make "Hit the Target" more complex by using target numbers in the range from 1 to 1000 and allowing the addition or subtraction of more numbers, such as 1, 2, 3, 5, 10, 15, 20, and 100. For games with larger numbers, you may want to have students use calculators.

Discussion

"Hit the Target" can give practice with addition and subtraction. Throughout the year, game sheets can be left in a folder in a game center for students to use during their free time. The game can also be sent home for students to play with their families.

As students gain more expertise with the game, they will become adept at considering alternative plans in light of what their opponents may do. This antecedent-consequence thinking is an important reasoning skill.

"All students should ... use a variety of methods and tools to compute, including objects, mental computation, estimation, paper and pencil, and calculators."
(NCTM 2000, p. 78)

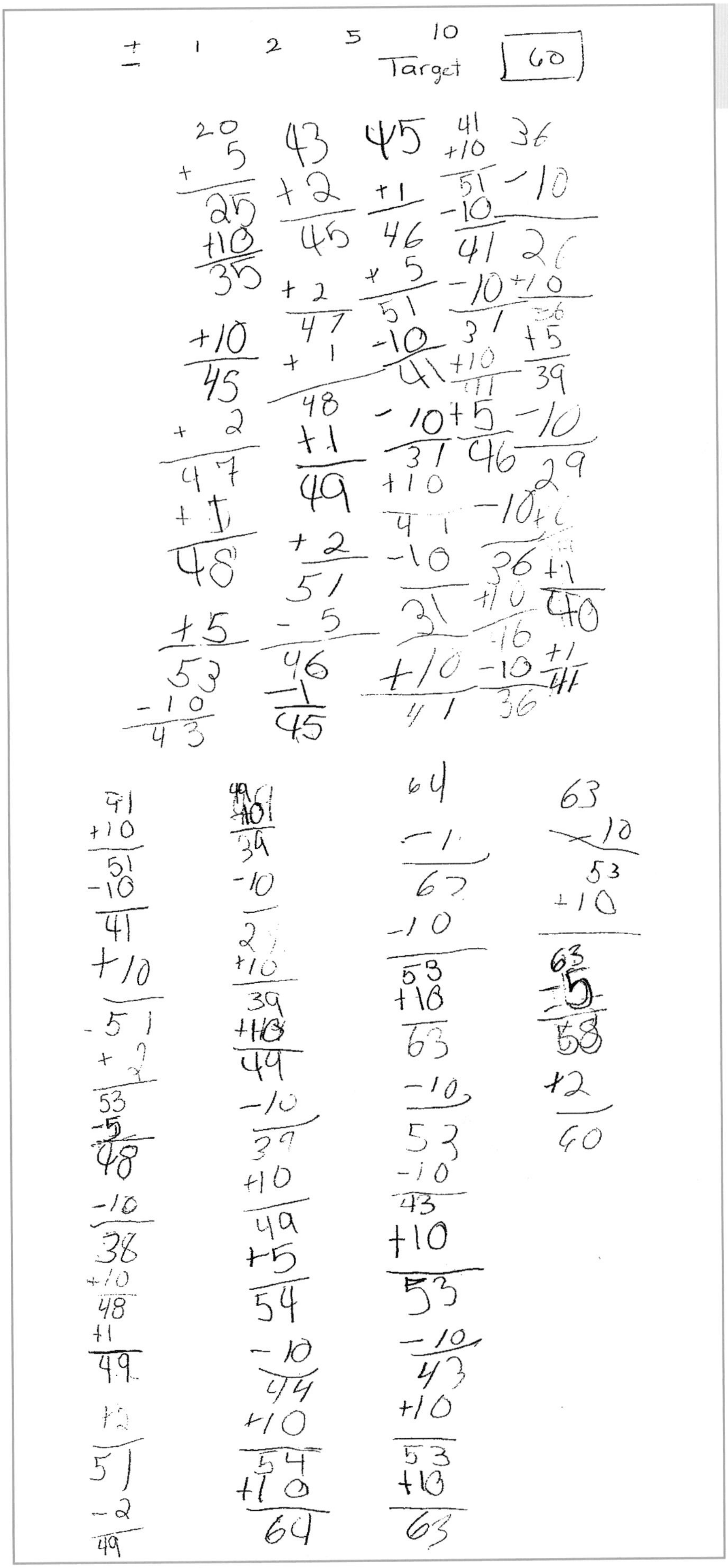

Fig. **3.3.**

Sample game sheet from students for "Hit the Target."

± | 1 | 2 | 5 | 10 Target [60]

```
    20
  + 5          43      45     41        36
 ─────        +2      +1    +10
   25          45      46     51      -10
  +10         +2      +5    -10        26
   35         ───    ───   -10+10
              47      51     31      36
  +10         +1     -10   +10+10     +5
   45        ───    ───   41        39
   +2         48     -10+5   -10
  ───        +1     31     46      29
   47        ───   +10
   +1         49    41     -10+10
  ───        +2    -10    36      +1
   48        ───   ───   +10      40
   +5         51    31   -16
  ───        -5        +10  -10+1
   53        46   +10  -10  41
  -10       ───   ───   36
  ───        45   41
   43
```

```
  41       49           64      63
 +10      +10          -1      -10
 ───      ───          ──      53
  51       39          62      +10
 -10      -10          -10    ───
 ───      ───          ──     63
  41       22          53      -5
 +10      +10         +10     ───
 ───      ───         ───     58
  51       39          63      +2
  +2      +10         -10     ───
 ───      ───          ──      60
  53       49          53
  -5      -10         -10
 ───      ───          ──
  48       39          43
 -10      +10         +10
 ───      ───         ───
  38       49          53
 +10      +5          -10
 ───      ───          ──
  48       54          43
  +1      -10         +10
 ───      ───         ───
  49       44          53
  +2      +10         +10
 ───      ───         ───
  51       54          63
  -2      +10
 ───      ───
  49       64
```

One-Out

Grades 1–2

Summary

In small groups, students play an addition game in which they mentally add 1, 2, 3, 4, 5, or 6 to one- or two-digit numbers.

Goal

- Add a one-digit number mentally to a one- or two-digit number

Prior Knowledge

- Counting to 50
- Knowing basic facts for adding and subtracting

Materials

- Two number cubes, each numbered 1, 2, 3, 4, 5, 6
- Paper and a pencil for each student

Activity

Engage

Draw four horizontal lines in a column on the chalkboard for students to copy (see illustration). Tell them to leave enough room between their lines that they can write numbers on the lines.

Introduce the game "One-Out" to the class by having two studenets play:

- Let each player roll the number cube in turn and identify the number facing up. This will be the player's starting number.

- Have each player roll the cube again in turn, identifying the new number, adding it mentally to the first number, and announcing the sum.

- Let the players continue rolling, mentally adding to their previous sum and announcing their new sums until someone rolls a 1.

At this point, remind the students that the name of the game is "One-Out," and explain that 1 is a powerful number in the game. Tell the students that players can have a 1 as a starting number, but after that, whenever someone rolls a 1, everyone loses all the points for the round and must record a zero for the round. However, there is a way to avoid getting a zero as a score for a round.

If a student wants a higher score than zero for a round, he or she may "freeze" a sum as it is increasing, before anyone rolls a 1. Any student who wants to freeze a score, says, "Freeze," and records that last sum as his or her score for the round. The round continues for players who have not yet frozen a score.

Thus, a round may end in one of two ways—

- with the rolling of a 1, or
- when all the students have frozen a score before anyone rolls a 1.

"All students should ... use a variety of methods and tools to compute, including objects, mental computation, estimation, paper and pencil, and calculators."

(NCTM 2000, p. 78)

All students are back in the game for each subsequent round.

Play continues for four rounds. After four rounds, students find the sum of their scores for the rounds. The student with the greatest sum for the four rounds wins.

Explore

Have your students play the game in groups of three or four, using these rules. Each student should draw four horizontal lines on a piece of paper. Have each group decide who will roll first, and let them take turns rolling the number cube to get their starting numbers. Players will then take turns rolling the number cube and adding the number rolled to the previous total. As in the demonstration, a player continues accumulating points for a round until he or she decides to freeze his or her score or until someone rolls a 1, ending the round, and the game continues for four rounds.

Extend

Provide students with variations on the game, or encourage them to modify a rule. For example, they can modify the game in the following ways:

* Increasing the number of rounds to five or six
* Using two number cubes, and declaring that a 1 on either cube ends the round
* Using two number cubes, and declaring that a sum of 7 on the cubes ends the round
* Using two number cubes, and declaring that doubles on the cubes end the round

Discussion

With one number cube, the expected probability of rolling a 1 is 1 out of 6. In practice, the actual occurrence of a 1 can vary

"It is not necessary to wait for students to fully develop place-value understandings before giving them opportunities to solve problems with two- and three-digit numbers." (NCTM 2000, p. 82)

dramatically. To eliminate disappointment among the students, some teachers use an "exception" rule: If all players have their starting numbers and then the first number rolled is 1, the student can roll again. Some rounds may continue for a long time without a 1 appearing. This means that students will be adding larger numbers, and this is a desirable outcome.

Conclusion

This chapter has provided students with opportunities to explore addition and subtraction while developing fact strategies, mental mathematics, estimation, and two-digit computation. The strategies that students begin to develop through activities such as those in chapter 3 build a foundation for computational fluency.

NAVIGATING *through* NUMBER *and* OPERATIONS

Looking Back and Looking Ahead

By the end of grade 2, students should be proficient at counting by ones, twos, fives, and tens. They should be able to count collections of objects and recognize that the count remains the same regardless of the size, shape, color, or function of the objects or the distance between any two objects. Students should be able to represent two- and three-digit numbers in different ways with place-value materials, and they should be able to identify the values of their digits. They should also be able to compare and order sets of two- and three-digit numbers.

During the early years, students explore different representations of simple fractions. By the end of grade 2, they should be able to identify and name one-half, one-third, and one-fourth of a region. They should be able to read and match symbols (1/2) with word names (*one-half*) and with pictures showing parts and regions.

In grades 3–5, students will extend their understanding of place value to represent multidigit whole numbers in different ways. They will learn to recognize fractions as parts of regions and as parts of groups. They will learn to generate equivalent fractions. They will also learn the relationships among equivalent forms of fractions, decimals, and percents.

Young students explore the meaning of addition (joining) and several meanings of subtraction (removing or "taking away" a subset, comparing, and finding the missing addend or answering the question, "How many more are needed?"), and they learn to compute sums and differences. They are introduced to multiplication as repeated addition, and they use skip counting to find, for example, the number of chips in four groups of two ("Two, 4, 6, 8; there are 8 chips"). They explore division as "sharing equally." By the end of grade 2, students should be able to add

See "Developing Computational Fluency with Whole Numbers," (Russell 2000) on the CD-ROM for ideas about connecting and assessing understanding and procedures in all the elementary grades.

or subtract with single-digit numbers and know when to add or subtract in problem situations.

In grades 3–5, students develop an understanding of the different meanings of multiplication and division, identify the relationships among operations (for example, division as repeated subtraction), and multiply and divide with whole numbers, decimals, and fractions. The activities in this next grade band emphasize estimating sums, differences, products, and quotients.

NAVIGATING through NUMBER and OPERATIONS

Appendix

Blackline Masters and Solutions

Eight Ducks

Navigating through Number and Operations in Prekindergarten–Grade 2

"All in Order" Game Sheet

Name _____

Round 1

_____

_____

_____

_____

    Smallest Number

    Second Number

    Third Number

    Greatest Number

Correct Order

_____

_____

_____

_____

Score _____

Round 2

_____

_____

_____

_____

    Smallest Number

    Second Number

    Third Number

    Greatest Number

Correct Order

_____

_____

_____

_____

Score _____

Round 3

_____

_____

_____

_____

    Smallest Number

    Second Number

    Third Number

    Greatest Number

Correct Order

_____

_____

_____

_____

Score _____

Total _____

"Fraction Concentration" Cards

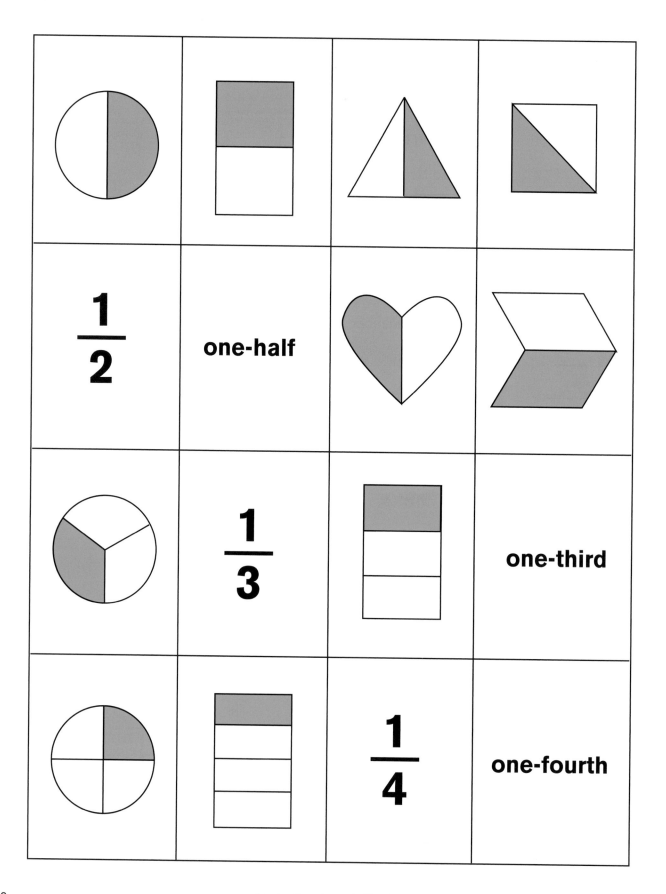

Frames

Name _____

Five-Frame

Ten-Frame

One Parking Lot

Name _____

Navigating through Number and Operations in Prekindergarten–Grade 2

Two Parking Lots

Name _____

Game Cards for "Flip Two"

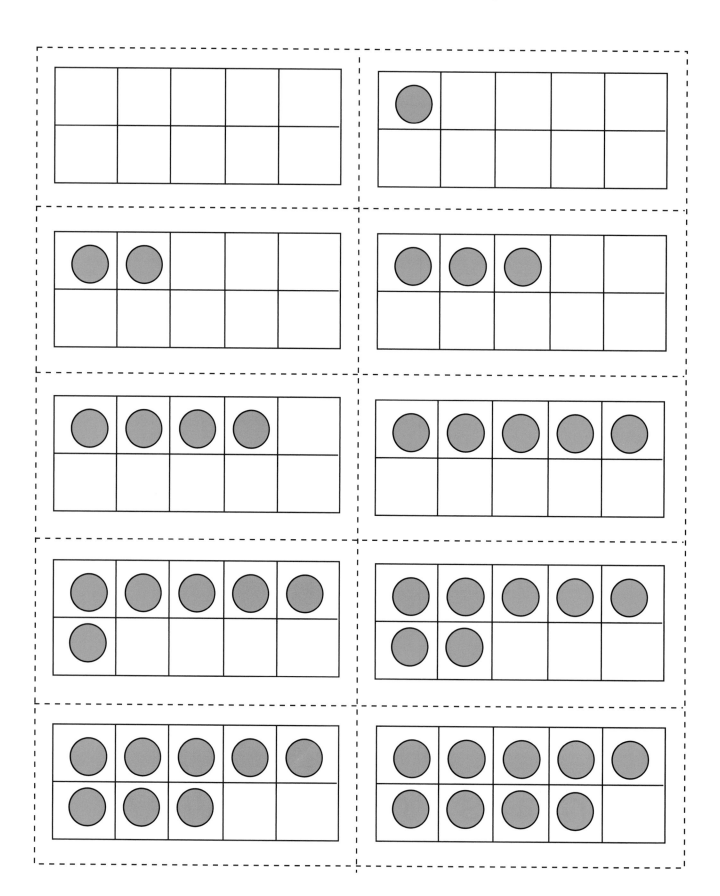

Gorilla's Lunch Menu A

Names _____

_____

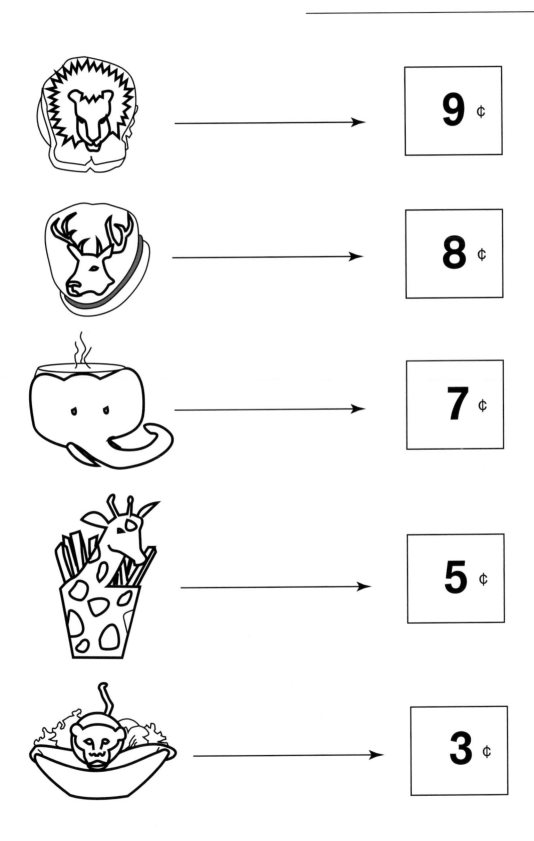

Gorilla's Lunch Menu B

Names _____

_____

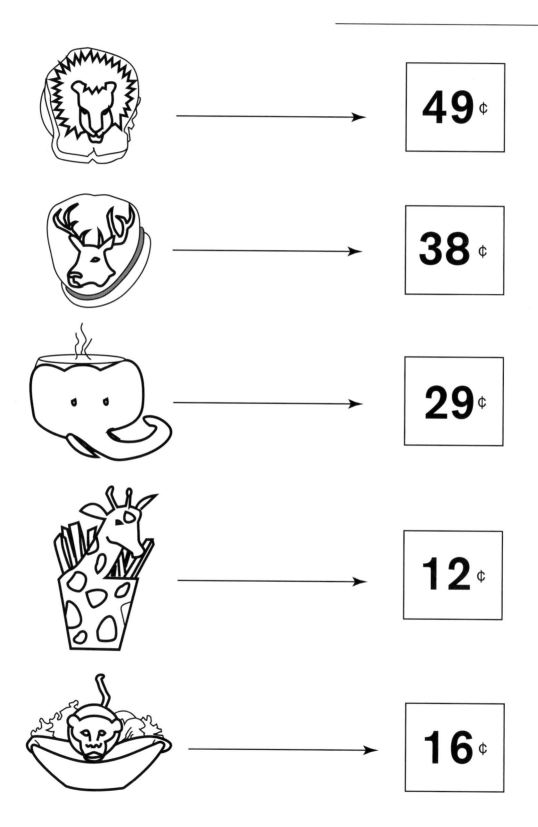

Navigating through Number and Operations in Prekindergarten–Grade 2

How Much?

Names _____

_____

1.  + [lion] = ▢

2. [giraffe] + [elephant] = ▢

3. [giraffe] + [elephant] + [monkey] = ▢

4. [deer] + [monkey] = ▢

How Much? (continued)

You pay with [   ] .

5. How much change do you get for a [monkey bowl] ? _____

6. How much change do you get for a [deer head] ? _____

7. How much more does [deer head] cost than [giraffe fries] costs? _____

8. How much more does [elephant] cost than [monkey bowl] costs? _____

9. What two items cost [   ] together? _____

_____

Valuable Art

Name _____

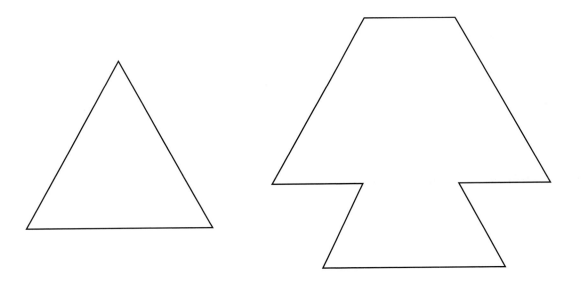

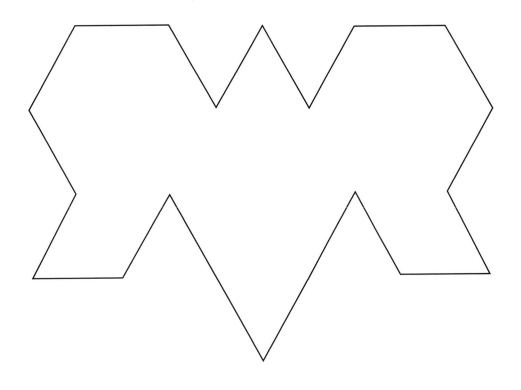

Game Board for "Four in a Row"

Name _____

46	25	20	31	14
8	100	53	121	82
37	70	83	32	53
59	43	14	52	44
89	112	21	91	15

Number Box A

41   20

9

3   32

Number Box B

50   11

80

5   12

"Hit the Target" Game Sheet

Names_____

Target Number [ ] (range: 50 to 100)   Starting number [ ] (range: 0–30)

Plus or minus 1, 2, 5, or 10

Solutions for "How Much?"

			Menu A	Menu B
1.	(deer) + (elephant) =		17¢	87¢
2.	(giraffe fries) + (elephant soup) =		12¢	41¢
3.	(giraffe fries) + (elephant soup) + (monkey salad) =		15¢	57¢
4.	(deer) + (monkey salad) =		11¢	54¢

You pay with 10¢ (Menu A) or $1.00 (Menu B).

		Menu A	Menu B
5.	How much change do you get for a monkey salad?	7¢	84¢
6.	How much change do you get for a deer hamburger?	2¢	62¢
7.	How much more does a deer hamburger cost than giraffe french fries cost?	3¢	26¢
8.	How much more does elephant soup cost than monkey salad costs?	4¢	13¢
9.	What two items cost 15¢ (Menu A) or 67¢ (Menu B) together?		

Navigating through Number and Operations in Prekindergarten–Grade 2

References

Carpenter, Thomas P., Deborah A. Carey, and Vicky L. Kouba. "A Problem-Solving Approach to the Operations." In *Mathematics for the Young Child*, edited by Joseph N. Payne, pp. 111–31. Reston, Va.: National Council of Teachers of Mathematics, 1990.

Carpenter, Thomas P., Elizabeth Fennema, Megan Franke, Linda Levi, and Susan Empson. *Children's Mathematics: Cognitively Guided Instruction.* Portsmouth, N.H.: Heinemann, 1999.

Carpenter, Thomas P., and James M. Moser. "The Acquisition of Addition and Subtraction Concepts in Grades One through Three." *Journal for Research in Mathematics Education* 15 (May 1984): 179–202.

Ehlert, Lois. *Fish Eyes: A Book You Can Count On.* New York: Red Wagon Books, 2001.

Findell, Carol R., Marian Small, Mary Cavanagh, Linda Dacey, Carole E. Greenes, and Linda Jensen Sheffield. *Navigating through Geometry in Prekindergarten–Grade 2. Principles and Standards for School Mathematics* Navigations Series. Reston, Va.: National Council of Teachers of Mathematics, 2001.

Fuson, Karen C. "Research on Whole Number Addition and Subtraction." In *Handbook of Research on Mathematics Teaching and Learning*, edited by Douglas A. Grouws, pp. 243–75. New York: Macmillan, 1992.

Fuson, Karen C., Laura Grandau, and Patricia A. Sugiyama. "Achievable Numerical Understandings for All Young Children." *Teaching Children Mathematics* 7 (May 2001): 522–26.

Ginsburg, Herbert, Alice Klein, and Prentice Starkey. "The Development of Children's Mathematical Knowledge: Connecting Research with Practice." In *Handbook of Child Psychology*, 5th ed., vol. 4, *Child Psychology in Practice*, edited by Irving E. Sigel and K. Ann Renninger, pp. 401–76. New York: John Wiley & Sons, 1998.

Hankes, Judith E. "An Alternative to Basic-Skills Remediation." *Teaching Children Mathematics* 2 (April 1996): 452–58.

Kline, Kate. "Helping at Home." *Teaching Children Mathematics* 5 (April 1999): 456–60.

Mathematics Learning Study Committee. "Developing Proficiency with Whole Numbers." Chap. 6 in *Adding It Up: Helping Children Learn Mathematics*, edited by Jeremy Kilpatrick, Jane Swafford, and Bradford Findell. Washington, D.C.: National Academy Press, 2001.

McCloskey, Robert. *Make Way for Ducklings.* New York: Viking Press, 1941.

Miura, Irene T. "The Influence of Language on Mathematical Representations." In *The Roles of Representation in School Mathematics*, 2001 Yearbook of the National Council of Teachers of Mathematics, edited by Albert A. Cuoco, pp. 53–62. Reston, Va.: National Council of Teachers of Mathematics, 2001.

National Council of Teachers of Mathematics (NCTM). *Principles and Standards for School Mathematics.* Reston, Va.: NCTM, 2000.

Richardson, Kathy. "Too Easy for Kindergarten and Just Right for First Grade." *Teaching Children Mathematics* 3 (April 1997): 432–37.

Russell, Susan Jo. "Developing Computational Fluency with Whole Numbers." *Teaching Children Mathematics* 7 (November 2000): 154–58.

Watanabe, Tad. "Ben's Understanding of One-Half." *Teaching Children Mathematics* 2 (April 1996): 460–64.

Suggested Reading

Baroody, Arthur J., and Jesse L. M. Wilkins. "The Development of Informal Counting, Number, and Arithmetic Skills and Concepts." In *Mathematics in the Early Years*, edited by Juanita V. Copley, pp. 48–65. Reston, Va.: National Council of Teachers of Mathematics; Washington, D.C.: National Association for the Education of Young Children, 1999.

Bove, Sandra P. "Place Value: A Vertical Perspective." *Teaching Children Mathematics* 1 (May 1995): 542–46.

Cavanagh, Mary. *Math to Learn*. Wilmington, Mass.: Great Source Education Group, 2002.

Clements, Douglas, and Julie Sarama. "Standards for Preschoolers." *Teaching Children Mathematics* 7 (September 2000): 38–41.

Dacey, Linda Schulman, and Rebeka Eston. *Growing Mathematical Ideas in Kindergarten*. Sausalito, Calif.: Math Solutions Publications, 1999.

Fuson, Karen C. "Research on Learning and Teaching Addition and Subtraction of Whole Numbers." In *Analysis of Arithmetic for Mathematics Teaching*, edited by Gaea Leinhardt, Ralph Putnam, and Rosemary A. Hattrup, pp. 53–188. Hillsdale, N.J.: Lawrence Erlbaum Associates, 1992.

Fuson, Karen C., Diana Wearne, James C. Hiebert, Hanlie G. Murray, Pieter G. Human, Alwyn I. Olivier, Thomas P. Carpenter, and Elizabeth Fennema. "Children's Conceptual Structures for Multidigit Numbers and Methods of Multidigit Addition and Subtraction." *Journal for Research in Mathematics Education* 28 (March 1997): 130–62.

Gelman, Rochel, and C. R. Gallistel. *The Child's Understanding of Number*. Cambridge, Mass.: Harvard University Press, 1978.

Greenes, Carole. "Ready to Learn: Developing Young Children's Mathematical Powers." In *Mathematics in the Early Years*, edited by Juanita V. Copley, pp. 39–47. Reston, Va.: National Council of Teachers of Mathematics; Washington, D.C.: National Association for the Education of Young Children, 1999.

Greenes, Carole, Linda Schulman Dacey, and Rika Spungin. *Addition and Subtraction, Grade 1*. Hot Math Topics Series. Parsippany, N.J.: Dale Seymour Publications, 1999.

———. *Addition and Subtraction, Grade 2*. Hot Math Topics Series. Parsippany, N.J.: Dale Seymour Publications, 1999.

———. *Number Sense, Grade 1*. Hot Math Topics Series. Parsippany, N.J.: Dale Seymour Publications, 1999.

———. *About Money and Time, Grade 1*. Hot Math Topics Series. Parsippany, N.J.: Dale Seymour Publications, 2001.

Hiebert, James, and Mary Lindquist. "Developing Mathematical Knowledge in the Young Child." In *Mathematics for the Young Child*, edited by Joseph N. Payne, pp. 17–36. Reston, Va.: National Council of Teachers of Mathematics, 1990.

Hiebert, James, and Diana Wearne. "Links between Teaching and Learning Place Value with Understanding in First Grade." *Journal for Research in Mathematics Education* 23 (March 1992): 98–122.

Hope, Jack, and Marian Small. *Interactions 1*. Toronto: Ginn Publishing Co., 1993.

———. *Interactions K*. Toronto: Ginn Publishing Co., 1994.

———. *Interactions 2*. Toronto: Ginn Publishing Co., 1994.

Isaacs, Andrew C., and William M. Carroll. "Strategies for Basic-Facts Instruction." *Teaching Children Mathematics* 5 (May 1999): 508–15.

Ma, Liping. *Knowing and Teaching Elementary Mathematics: Teachers' Understanding of Fundamental Mathematics in China and the United States.* Mahwah, N.J.: Lawrence Erlbaum Associates, 1999.

McClain, Kay, and Paul Cobb. "Supporting Students' Ways of Reasoning about Patterns and Partitions." In *Mathematics in the Early Years*, edited by Juanita V. Copley, pp. 112–18. Reston, Va.: National Council of Teachers of Mathematics; Washington, D.C.: National Association for the Education of Young Children, 1999.

McIntosh, Alistair. "Teaching Mental Algorithms Constructively." In *The Teaching and Learning of Algorithms in School Mathematics*, 1998 Yearbook of the National Council of Teachers of Mathematics, edited by Lorna J. Morrow, pp. 44–48. Reston, Va.: National Council of Teachers of Mathematics, 1998.

Richardson, Kathy. *Developing Number Concepts.* 3 books. White Plains, N.Y.: Dale Seymour Publications, 1999.

Ron, Pilar. "My Family Taught Me This Way." In *The Teaching and Learning of Algorithms in School Mathematics*, 1998 Yearbook of the National Council Teachers of Mathematics, edited by Lorna J. Morrow, pp. 115–19. Reston, Va.: National Council of Teachers of Mathematics, 1998.

Steffe, Leslie P., and Paul Cobb. *Construction of Arithmetical Meanings and Strategies.* New York: Springer-Verlag, 1988.

Tang, Eileen P., and Herbert P. Ginsburg. "Young Children's Mathematical Reasoning: A Psychological View." In *Developing Mathematical Reasoning in Grades K–12*, 1999 Yearbook of the National Council of Teachers of Mathematics, edited by Lee V. Stiff, pp. 45–61. Reston, Va.: National Council of Teachers of Mathematics, 1999.

Thornton, Carol A. "Strategies for the Basic Facts." In *Mathematics for the Young Child*, edited by Joseph N. Payne, pp. 133–51. Reston, Va.: National Council of Teachers of Mathematics, 1990.

Van de Walle, John A. "Concepts of Number." In *Mathematics for the Young Child*, edited by Joseph N. Payne, pp. 63–87. Reston, Va.: National Council of Teachers of Mathematics, 1990.